Issues in Religion and Theology

8

Anthropological Approaches to the Old Testament

Wesley Toews, 1991

Issues in Religion and Theology

SERIES EDITORS

Titles in the series include:

Issues in Religion and Theology 8

Anthropological Approaches to the Old Testament

Edited with an Introduction by

BERNHARD LANG

FORTRESS PRESS | SPCK
Philadelphia | London

First published in Great Britain 1985
SPCK
Holy Trinity Church
Marylebone Road
London NW1 4DU

First published in the USA 1985
Fortress Press
2900 Queen Lane
Philadelphia
Pennsylvania 19129

Library of Congress Cataloging in Publication Data
Main entry under title:

Anthropological approaches to the Old Testament.

  (Issues in religion and theology; 8)
  Bibliography: p.
  Contents: Enslavement and the early Hebrew lineage
system/Franz Steiner—The sin of Cain/Isaac
Schapera—The Hebrew conception of corporate
personality/John W. Rogerson—[etc.]
  1. Bible. O.T.—Criticism, interpretation, etc.—
Addresses, essays, lectures. 2. Sociology, Biblical—
Addresses, essays, lectures. 3. Ethnology—Addresses,
essays, lectures. I. Lang, Bernhard, 1946– .
II. Series.
BS1192.A48 1985   221.6′7   84–48723
ISBN 0–8006–1771–1

British Library Cataloguing in Publication Data

Anthropological approaches to the Old Testament.—
  (Issues in religion and theology; no. 8)
  1. Bible O.T.—Criticism, interpretation, etc.
  2. Ethnology in the Bible
I. Lang, Bernhard   II. Series
221.9′5   BS1199.M2

ISBN 0–281–04172–5

Filmset by Northumberland Press Ltd, Gateshead
Printed in Great Britain by Richard Clay (The Chaucer Press) Ltd, Bungay, Suffolk

Contents

Contents

The Contributors

FRANZ STEINER (1909–52) was Lecturer in Social Anthropology at the University of Oxford. His book on *Taboo* was published after his early death.

ISAAC SCHAPERA is emeritus professor of Social Anthropology at the London School of Economics. Among his many books are *Khoisan Peoples of South Africa*, *Rainmaking Rites of Tswana Tribes*, and *Handbook of Tswana Law and Custom*.

JOHN W. ROGERSON is head of the Department of Biblical Studies in the University of Sheffield, England. His books include *Myth in Old Testament Interpretation* and *Anthropology and the Old Testament*.

THOMAS W. OVERHOLT is professor of Philosophy in the University of Wisconsin at Stevens Point. He is the author of *The Threat of Falsehood: A Study in Jeremiah*, and co-edited *Anthropological Perspectives on Old Testament Prophecy*.

BERNHARD LANG is professor of Religious Studies at the University of Paderborn, Germany. He is the author of *Monotheism and the Prophetic Minority: An Essay in Biblical History and Sociology* and editor of the *International Review of Biblical Studies*.

MARY DOUGLAS is Avalon Professor in Humanities at Northwestern University, Evanston, Illinois. Her famous books include *The Lele of Kasai*, *Purity and Danger*, *Natural Symbols* and *Implicit Meanings*.

MICHAEL P. CARROLL is professor of Sociology at the University of Western Ontario in London, Canada.

Sir EDMUND LEACH is emeritus professor of Social Anthropology at the University of Cambridge. Among his many publications are *Political Systems of Highland Burma*, *Rethinking Anthropology*, *Genesis as Myth*, and *Social Anthropology*.

DOUGLAS DAVIES is lecturer in the Department of Theology at the University of Nottingham, England. He recently published *Meaning and Salvation in Religious Studies*.

Acknowledgements

Franz Steiner, "Enslavement and the Early Hebrew Lineage System", is reprinted by permission from *Man* 54 (1954) 73–5. Copyright © 1954 by The Royal Anthropological Institute, London.

Isaac Schapera, "The Sin of Cain", is reprinted by permission from *Journal of the Royal Anthropological Institute* 85 (1955) 33–43. Copyright © 1955 by The Royal Anthropological Institute, London.

John W. Rogerson, "The Hebrew Conception of Corporate Personality", is reprinted by permission from *Journal of Theological Studies* 21 (1970) 1–16. Copyright © 1970 by Oxford University Press.

Thomas W. Overholt, "Prophecy: The Problem of Cross-Cultural Comparison", is reprinted by permission from *Semeia* 21 (1982) 55–78. Copyright © 1982 by the Society of Biblical Literature, Chico, CA.

Bernhard Lang, "The Social Organization of Peasant Poverty in Biblical Israel", is reprinted by permission from *Monotheism and the Prophetic Minority* (Sheffield: Almond Press, 1983) 114–27. Copyright © 1983 by The Almond Press, Sheffield.

Mary Douglas, "The Abominations of Leviticus", is reprinted by permission from *Purity and Danger* (London: Routledge & Kegan Paul, 1969) 41–57. Copyright © 1966 by Mary Douglas.

Michael P. Carroll, "One More Time: Leviticus Revisited", is reprinted by permission from *Archives européennes de sociologie* 19 (1978) 339–46. Copyright © by Archives européennes de sociologie, Musée de l'Homme, Paris.

Michael P. Carroll, "Genesis Restructured", is reprinted by permission from the author's paper, "Leach, Genesis, and Structural Analysis", in *American Ethnologist* 4 (1977) 663–77. Copyright © 1977 by American Anthropological Association, Washington.

Edmund Leach, "The Logic of Sacrifice", is reprinted by permission from *Culture and Communication* (Cambridge: Cambridge University Press, 1976) 81–93. Copyright © 1976 by Cambridge University Press.

Douglas Davies, "An Interpretation of Sacrifice in Leviticus", is reprinted by permission from *Zeitschrift für die alttestamentliche Wissenschaft* 89 (1977) 388–98. Copyright © 1977 by Walter de Gruyter & Co., Berlin.

Series Foreword

The Issues in Religion and Theology series intends to encompass a variety of topics within the general disciplines of religious and theological studies. Subjects are drawn from any of the component fields, such as biblical studies, systematic theology, ethics, history of Christian thought, and history of religion. The issues have all proved to be highly significant for their respective areas, and they are of similar interest to students, teachers, clergy, and general readers.

The series aims to address these issues by collecting and reproducing key studies, all previously published, which have contributed significantly to our present understandings. In each case, the volume editor introduces the discussion with an original essay which describes the subject and its treatment in religious and theological studies. To this editor has also fallen the responsibility of selecting items for inclusion – no easy task when one considers the vast number of possibilities. Together the essays are intended to present a balanced overview of the problem and various approaches to it. Each piece is important in the current debate, and any older publication included normally stands as a classical or seminal work which is still worth careful study. Readers unfamiliar with the issue should find that these discussions provide a good entrée, while more advanced students will appreciate having studies by some of the best specialists on the subject gathered together in one volume.

The editor has, of course, faced certain constraints: analyses too lengthy or too technical could not be included, except perhaps in excerpt form; the bibliography is not exhaustive; and the volumes in this series are being kept to a reasonable, uniform length. On the other hand, the editor is able to overcome the real problem of inaccessibility. Much of the best literature on a subject is often not readily available to readers, whether because it was first published in journals or books not widely circulated or because it was originally written in a language not read by all who would benefit from it. By bringing these and other studies together in this series, we hope to contribute to the general understanding of these key topics.

Series Foreword

The series editors and the publishers wish to express their gratitude to the authors and their original publishers whose works are reprinted or translated here, often with corrections from living authors. We are also conscious of our debt to members of the editorial advisory board. They have shared our belief that the series will be used on a wide scale, and they have therefore been prepared to spare much time and thought for the project.

DOUGLAS A. KNIGHT
ROBERT MORGAN

Abbreviations

AA	*American Anthropologist*
AE	*American Ethnologist*
AES	*Archives européennes de sociologie*
BJRL	*Bulletin of the John Rylands Library*
BN	*Biblische Notizen*
BSOAS	*Bulletin of the School of Oriental and African Studies*
BZAW	Beihefte zur Zeitschrift für die alttestamentliche Wissenschaft
CA	*Current Anthropology*
CBQ	*Catholic Biblical Quarterly*
CSSH	*Comparative Studies in Society and History*
ET	English translation/English translator
HTR	*Harvard Theological Review*
ICC	International Critical Commentary
JAAR	*Journal of the American Academy of Religion*
JBL	*Journal of Biblical Literature*
JETS	*Journal of the Evangelical Theological Society*
JNES	*Journal of Near Eastern Studies*
JRAI	*Journal of the Royal Anthropological Institute*
JSOT	*Journal for the Study of the Old Testament*
JTS	*Journal of Theological Studies*
OTL	Old Testament Library
SR	*Studies in Religion*
SUNT	Studien zur Umwelt des Neuen Testaments
TBü	Theologische Bücherei
TWNT	*Theologisches Wörterbuch zum Neuen Testament*, ed. G. Kittel, G. Friedrich (1933–79)
VT	*Vetus Testamentum*
VTSup	Vetus Testamentum, Supplements
WMANT	Wissenschaftliche Monographien zum Alten und Neuen Testament
ZAW	*Zeitschrift für die alttestamentliche Wissenschaft*

Introduction:
Anthropology as a New Model
for Biblical Studies

BERNHARD LANG

"I learnt more about the nature of God and our human predicament from the Nuer than I ever learnt at home", wrote Sir Edward Evans-Pritchard, one of the foremost British anthropologists of the last generation.[1] The Nuer were a cattle-herding African people in the southern Sudan. In 1930–6 Evans-Pritchard lived with them for some twelve months. He learned their language, studied their way of life, and became an expert on their ritual as well as their view of the world. Nuer religion, as this anthropologist saw it, shared many features with biblical religion, including a belief that can be described in monotheistic terms, a ritual which involves animal sacrifices, and prophets as prominent religious figures. Thus Nuer religion could provide the scholar with insights into his own Judeo-Christian tradition. Among the Nuer, asserted Evans-Pritchard, both the missionary and the anthropologist felt as if they were living in Old Testament times.[2] Can the encounter with a non-Western culture, especially one that reminds us of biblical times, really help us to understand the Bible?

In the nineteenth century biblical studies were the almost exclusive domain of theologians who transmitted their knowledge in church- or synagogue-sponsored seminaries and academic institutions. Most theologians knew some Hebrew and classical Greek, but their interest focused on biblical theology and history. The academic situation has radically changed since then. Biblical Hebrew is no longer the domain of theologians, but is now studied by experts on ancient Near-Eastern languages. To see students of English or comparative literature studying the Bible is now commonplace. Likewise social scientists, especially sociologists and anthropologists,

1

have become aware of the Bible as a storehouse of ethnographic data about an interesting non-Western culture – one that in fact is incorporated into our own history.

What are anthropologists doing, and what kinds of ethnographic data are they concerned with? The best way to explain what anthropology is all about is to describe what anthropologists do. In order to study other cultures – cultures outside their own – they try to get as close as possible to their subject of research. The principal way to do this is to learn the language of the people, live among them for an extended period of time, and join in their everyday activities.

Anthropologists call this method of research "participant observation". The term "observation" implies that the scholar should actually witness what he or she is writing about rather than rely on second-hand information received from travellers or untrained native informants. Major anthropologists of our century have lived with and written about: the Trobrianders in Melanesia (Bronislaw Malinowski), the Kwakiutl in British Columbia (Franz Boas), the peasants of a Mexican village (Robert Redfield), the Kachin in highland Burma (Edmund Leach) and, as we have seen, the Nuer in Africa. On the basis of participant observation a whole library of ethnography, i.e. "description of a people", was produced. Studied before the penetration by industrialism, a typical "ethnographic" society was marked by illiteracy or non-literacy, strong religious life, small-scale economy, and the importance of kinship connections in social, political, economic and religious networks.

Studies of individual societies are accompanied by works of a more comparative and theoretical nature. Kinship systems, modes of production, mythology, religious practices, political leadership (or its virtual absence), and even warfare are the aspects of life anthropologists discuss in traditional and, more recently, industrial societies. Thus the already immense library of ethnographical records is supplemented by an equally impressive number of exercises in anthropological theory. Some significant titles are: *The Elementary Forms of the Religious Life* (Emile Durkheim), *The Gift* (Marcel Mauss), *The Elementary Structures of Kinship* (Claude Lévi-Strauss), *African Political Systems* (ed. Meyer Fortes and E. E. Evans-Pritchard), *Peasant Society and Culture* (Robert Redfield), and *Ecstatic Religion* (Ioan M. Lewis).

The ancient Israelite and early Jewish society in which the Bible originated does not exist any more. In spite of its impressive and all-pervasive impact on later social and religious development it must be said that biblical culture is a dead civilization, as dead as the cultures of ancient Egypt or classical Greece. Although biblical Hebrew can be learned, "participant observation" of ancient Hebrew culture is no longer possible. The Bible does not belong to the immediate domain of anthropological inquiry. Anthropologists study living people, not books.

Happily enough, however, anthropologists have been interested in the Bible as well as other ancient literatures, and biblical scholars as well as classicists[3] have looked to anthropology for insights. Both sides discovered that ancient cultures share certain characteristics with some of the societies studied by anthropologists. When reading the Bible the anthropologist draws upon his knowledge of other traditional cultures. He or she may become aware of certain details of ancient culture that may well escape the general reader and even the biblical specialist. The anthropologist's trained eyes may "see" things others simply miss. "In a working life of some thirty-five years spent for the most part in West African villages as an ethnographer and a clinical psychiatrist", explains one author,

> I have become thoroughly familiar not only with certain mental phenomena seldom seen in Europe (such as 'spirit possession') but also with some almost universal primitive customs ... On re-reading the biblical narratives, I am now able to recognize many an item of behaviour there recorded as something which I myself have *seen*.[4]

The essays included in this volume reflect biblical research done by professional anthropologists and, to a lesser extent, research by biblical scholars involved with anthropological study. All of these articles have been published in the past three decades during a period of renewed interest in the anthropological approach to biblical studies. While a number of authors study biblical culture as they would any other non-industrial society, others take a more theoretical approach. We will first introduce the essays which follow the "comparative ethnography" approach, and then those which study systems of classification or use the methods of structural anthropology. A final section will move beyond this collection of essays in discussing the present state of the anthropological approach to OT studies.

Comparative Ethnography: The Past

In an undeveloped form comparative ethnography is as old as the discovery of the New World by European explorers. In 1550 the

German traveller Hans Staden reported that the Tupinamba people living on the coast of what is now Brazil had a story which closely resembled the biblical account of the deluge. One generation later the French philosopher Michel de Montaigne collected a whole series of such parallels he found in the fashionable travel books of his days. He concluded that "these vaine shadowes of our religion, which are seene in some of these examples, witnesse the dignity and divinity therof".[5]

It is no wonder that later authors compiled many-volumed works which quote such information from all over the world, but particularly from the Arabic-speaking countries of the Middle East which they call the Bible lands.[6] Some were convinced that in these countries Mohammed's monotheism was the only major innovation since the days of the Bible, and even this was ultimately derived from ancient Jewish belief. The anthropological myth of the static, immovable East can still be seen in contemporary Bible illustrations which often assimilate Moses to a Bedouin sheikh by furnishing him with a long kaftan and a picturesque turban. Gustave Doré was one of these "orientalizing" artists whose work is still reproduced and well-known. In his *Letters Concerning the Study of Divinity* Johann Gottfried Herder insisted that oriental travel reports were much better guides to the Bible than the dry exegetical commentaries used by his eighteenth-century contemporaries.[7] The traveller who had first-hand experience of the biblical land and lore would be the one who captured the true oriental spirit. It would be in the stories and anecdotes of the East that the Bible would come to life.

Two nineteenth-century visitors to the Middle East were dissatisfied with this anecdotal way of using evidence from the Bible lands and devised more systematic methods. The first of them was Edward Robinson (1794–1863), an American biblical scholar who in 1838 and 1852 extensively travelled in Palestine and adjacent countries. He was interested not in anecdotes illustrating manners and customs found in the Bible, but in topography and geography. Not conversant with Arabic, he was accompanied by interpreters and guides willing to escort him to places of no particular interest to the ordinary pilgrim or merchant. Thus he was able to identify many modern settlements and abandoned ruins with places mentioned in the Bible. Robinson became one of the founding figures of Palestinian archaeology.

The Scottish scholar William Robertson Smith (1846–94) had interests very different from those of Robinson. As an Arabic and biblical scholar he joined the lively debate on social and religious

4

origins which dominated the intellectual atmosphere of late Victorian society. Inspired by Darwin, people thought in terms of evolution. One fashionable idea was that many characteristics of earlier and more primitive societies survived in later and more sophisticated civilizations. Drawing upon his experience of the East, anthropological writings, and German biblical criticism, Robertson Smith tried to reconstruct the earliest stage of Semitic society and Hebrew religion.

According to Robertson Smith, under the surface of sophisticated Islamic civilization traces of the earlier stages of Semitic culture could be found. In his *Lectures on the Religion of the Semites* (2nd edn 1894)[8] he presented the distinction between an earlier phase of a clan-centred religion of ecstatic joy and a later phase of a priest-centred religion of fear based on elaborate expiatory rituals of sacrifice. Originally, Robertson Smith believed, Semitic religion was based on a joyous bond between a clan and its god celebrated in sacrificial meals in which every member of the clan shared. The meal allowed for communion with both the deity and the other members of the clan, and was felt to promote group solidarity and cohesion. The clan deity was seen as a member of the clan itself, an idea Robertson Smith borrowed from totemism. The god also was the sacrificial victim ritually eaten.

Stripped of outdated theories which are not crucial for the argument, Robertson Smith has still a message for the modern student of the OT. From him one can learn that there are (at least) two forms of Hebrew religion. Most scholars, though, would not place them in temporal sequence. They would rather define them as belonging to different social worlds: one type a family or private ritual, and the other type a clericalized temple worship promoted by the monarchy. Furthermore, Robertson Smith can direct our attention to the more important fact that many ritual activities performed by communities serve to express and strengthen group cohesion and solidarity. This insight as such was not new, and had been anticipated by Maimonides in the Middle Ages.[9] What was new, however, was the sophistication with which it was used in analysing religious symbolism and the function of ritual. One of the founding fathers of modern sociology, Emile Durkheim, acknowledged his indebtedness to Robertson Smith when he took up and developed the idea in his monumental *Elementary Forms of the Religious Life* (1912).

While the work of Robertson Smith is still worth reading this cannot be said of Sir James Frazer's *Folk-Lore in the Old Testament* without some qualification. Frazer's three massive volumes published in 1918 are loosely connected collections of ethnographic parallels illustrating biblical themes such as creation and the fall, the great flood, cross-cousin marriage, and the injunction not to seethe a kid in its mother's milk. Not infrequently he piles up parallels only dimly relevant to the point at hand. Smith's emphasis on ancient Semitic culture is almost completely abandoned in favour of the assumption that the biblical record preserves traces of an earlier age when the Semites were "savages". Because Semitic culture has evolved out of savagery (as any other culture), one can see savagery within the Bible. Although biblical man has left this stage far behind, relics and survivals which betray the spirit of earlier times can be recovered by applying the comparative method.

In many cases Frazer postulates the existence of earlier versions of biblical stories. One example may suffice. On the basis of tales widely diffused throughout the world, he reconstructs how the original story of man's fall (Gen. 3) probably ran.[10] He argues that it is really a combination of two stories called "The Perverted Message" and "The Cast Skin". These were primitive endeavours to solve the mystery of death. God intended men and women to be immortal and so sent the serpent to tell them to eat of the tree of life and live for ever. On the way the serpent bethought himself to pervert the message, and accordingly persuaded them to eat of the wrong tree, while he himself ate of the tree of immortality. Hence the serpent by casting its skin is able to rejuvenate itself and become immortal. While Frazer's reference to the motif of the cast skin is quite to the point, there is simply no evidence for the perverted message in the biblical account or in any other creation story of the ancient Middle East.

It must be emphasized that Frazer's somewhat rudimentary notion of survivals is no longer considered useful by anthropologists. Biblical scholars are reluctant to comment on "biblical" themes not found in the actual text. Frazer had discredited the comparative method, and more than one generation passed before scholars resumed this approach. As anthropologists they would consider themselves as disciples of Robertson Smith (and Durkheim) rather than of Frazer.

Comparative Ethnography: The Present

At this point we can comment on the essays included in this collection. After Frazer the first to apply the comparative method to the OT were anthropologists whose Jewish background provided them with some knowledge of both the Hebrew language and biblical history. Perhaps it is no coincidence, too, that Franz Steiner and Isaac Schapera, our first two authors, were both Africanists teaching in Britain. Even the casual reader of Evans-Pritchard's *Nuer Religion* cannot fail to notice how frequently the Oxford professor refers to the OT to explain certain beliefs or ritual customs.[11] So if the Bible could elucidate African practices and institutions, why could not African society illuminate biblical studies?

Franz Steiner's paper, presented at the International Congress of Anthropological and Ethnological Sciences in 1948, uses rules that operate in African lineage systems to clarify a passage of the Joseph story. He argues that in Gen. 47—48 Joseph and Jacob are not conceived of as son and father but as two independent partners. This occurred because Joseph had been sold into slavery, losing his kinship connections as well as his filial obligations. Consequently, Joseph's sons have to be incorporated into Jacob's lineage from which they had been excluded. Only on the basis of a legitimizing process can they rightfully become the descendants of Jacob/Israel.

In his 1954 Frazer lecture Schapera also uses African kinship networks to clarify why Cain was protected by God rather than punished by his family. On the basis of comparative evidence he suggests that if the deceased and the assassin are immediate kin feud-vengeance is impossible. One possible solution would be to expel the murderer, and this happened with Cain.

Rogerson does not suggest new analogies found in ethnographic writing but rather gives us a glimpse of the ongoing debate about the "primitive mentality" which supposedly is different from ours. While authors such as Max Weber concluded that Hebrew thought is the very inspiration of the Western rational mind, others compare it to the primitive mind as described by L. Lévy-Bruhl. It was not enough to point out that in biblical times a whole group could be made responsible for the action of the head of the group or one of its members. Scholars started to speculate about primitive man's "defective sense of individuality", and the resulting absorption into a social body H. W. Robinson called the "corporate personality". Rogerson shows that biblical scholarship, as well as anthropology, can well do without such doubtful speculation.[12]

Rogerson's critique of Lévy-Bruhlian assumptions can be applied fruitfully to other areas of biblical research where the primitive mentality approach is still commonplace. It is generally argued, for instance, that the symbolic acts performed by angry Hebrew prophets were thought to be almost automatically effective in producing national misfortune. This view has now come under an attack similar to the one voiced by Rogerson.[13] Far from being magical engineerings based on pre-logical thought, most of these prophetic acts served as challenging propaganda comparable to modern street theatre. Rogerson has put the detection of outdated or problematic anthropological assumptions on the permanent agenda of biblical scholarship.

Overholt's essay is an attempt to analyse cross-culturally the interaction between prophet and society. He devises a model and applies it to two prophetic figures: the biblical Jeremiah and Handsome Lake, a Seneca Indian of the late eighteenth and early nineteenth centuries. What can be compared cross-culturally is not so much the content of the prophetic message as the religious and social mechanisms by which it is produced. Such mechanisms include revelatory experience, expectations of the audience, prophet–audience interaction, and the like.

In the Lang article the concept of "peasant society" is borrowed from economic anthropology and applied to the social situation presupposed by the Book of Amos. I argue that the ancient Israelite peasants were often exploited by urban landlords, merchants or money-lenders according to a strategy Hans Bobek described as the "rent capitalism" typical of the traditional Middle East. Like modern capitalism this system separates labour and ownership of the means of production. But unlike its modern successor rent capitalism does not produce increasing profits. The pre-modern capitalist uses the small rents in order to live in luxury rather than to develop his capital by reinvesting the income.

The Bible in Purity and Danger

Comparative ethnography tries to elucidate biblical texts by comparing them to what is known from other non-industrial societies. Mary Douglas, however, uses the Bible to cope with problems posed by anthropological research. While doing her fieldwork among the Lele in Central Africa, Douglas experienced the lives of women as they cooked, divided food, talked about illness, babies, and proper care of the body. To her Lele women seemed to be "a lot of squeamish, hypochondriac old maids, worried about absurdly elaborate etiquette and superstitious hygiene".[14] By studying Lele food and table manners she became more and more conscious of a central anthropological problem, that of "pollution".

What started as an attempt at making sense out of unsystematic field notes about seemingly disparate "superstitions" developed into a major exercise in anthropological theory.

Douglas' chapter on "The Abominations of Leviticus" is part of a book on the concepts of taboo and pollution. Such avoidance behaviour exists in many societies and religions, especially in Judaism and Hinduism. Douglas explores what accounts for what is either pure or impure (and hence dangerous) in a given society. In *Purity and Danger* she argues that pollution is not just characteristic of "primitive" societies, but a universal concept which can be explained by a general rule. Whatever is outside or on the margin of a system of classification, says Douglas, is polluted and thus impure, taboo, and forbidden to be touched or consumed.

The concept of "system" is crucial for understanding pollution which must be seen as a "relative idea". To quote the author's "Western" example:

> Shoes are not dirty in themselves, but it is dirty to place them on the dining-table; food is not dirty in itself, but it is dirty to leave cooking utensils in the bedroom, or food bespattered on clothing ... In short, our pollution behaviour is the reaction which condemns any object or idea likely to confuse or contradict cherished classifications.[15]

For this purpose, "dirt" is re-defined as "matter out of place". The "matter" is out there in the world, but it is we who define the place. Thus dirt is an entirely sociocentric concept.

Another example of pollution is taken from the Bible. In her analysis of Jewish dietary laws, specifically the taboo against eating pork, she argues that the prohibited "abominations" of Leviticus are animals which appear anomalous in the Israelite classification system. Proper land animals such as cattle and sheep have cloven hooves and chew their cud. Pigs are cloven-hoofed and do not chew their cud. The camel, on the other hand, is cud-chewing, but does not have cloven hooves. These animals are therefore outside the known categories, and hence impure. By avoiding what in nature challenges God's order, people confirm that order. Through a dietary observance God is made holy – separate and whole. By respecting God's established order Israelite society affirms its own cultural identity, just as we affirm ours by putting things where they belong, utensils back into the kitchen, and our shoes under the table.

All this is very suggestive and straightforward. But there remains a problem. Douglas translates native views of pollution into a more abstract, coherent system. That certain things should be separated and everything kept in its proper place sounds quite well, but it does not explain very much. Who or what defines the "proper place" for things? Douglas gives hardly any hints on how the system of proper places came into being. Like Frazer she suggests that the Israelites did not eat creatures which did not resemble sheep and cattle, their most common domestic animals. Sheep and cattle would be a pastoralist's appropriate model for true land animals that may be consumed.[16] There are social ramifications that remain unexplored.

In two papers not included here, Mary Douglas presents her second thoughts on "The Abominations of Leviticus".[17] She makes more explicit that according to Durkheim the properties of classification systems are derived from social systems in which they are used. The symbolic universe reflects the social world. Hence, the Levitical insistence on the clear distinction between the polluting and the non-polluting must be seen as a part of a larger pattern of social behaviour. This society uses clear, tight defining lines to distinguish between two classes of human beings, the Israelites and the rest. Since every outsider is considered a threat to society and religion, some parts of nature are singled out to represent an abominable intruder who breaches boundaries that should be kept intact.

Among the various critiques and evaluations of Douglas' treatment of biblical dietary prohibitions, Michael Carroll's paper stands as the most suggestive.[18] While accepting Douglas' general approach, he points out certain difficulties in her handling of flying creatures. Rather than representing unusual animal categories, carrion-eating birds and "carnivorous" flying insects blur the boundary between meat-eating man and plant-eating animal, and are therefore classified as unclean. As a good structuralist Carroll reduces the man/animal opposition to yet a more basic one, that of culture and nature.

Structural Anthropology

By drawing on linguistic analogy structuralists endeavour to look at things from the "grammatical" point of view. They want to find out the rules and laws which underlie kinship systems, govern mythical narrative, and inspire religious ritual. While structuralists share this interest with non-structuralist anthropologists, the followers of Lévi-Strauss develop their own ideas about reducing these laws to a relatively small set of "elementary structures" or "models" that make up a basic grammar. One such model is the "binary opposition" of nature and culture we met in Carroll's paper. Claude Lévi-Strauss, the founding father of this approach, saw this grammar as consisting of "the principles through which the human mind operates".

Lévi-Strauss was reluctant to exercise his skill in biblical studies, and so it was the British anthropologist Sir Edmund Leach who first applied structuralism to biblical material. In his 1961 essay, "Lévi-Strauss in the Garden of Eden",[19] he examined the first four chapters of Genesis. Since then Leach has published two collections of papers on the Bible.[20] Most authors responding to the work of Leach are very critical of his exegesis, his assumption of homosexual incest between Cain and Abel being only one example of weird speculation. Since structural readings of texts are often as complicated as they are controversial, this collection includes only papers which can be read and appreciated by even the uninitiated.

Carroll's essay challenges Leach's conclusions on Genesis 1—4. In the second part which is printed here, the author shows that by applying certain rules of transformation one can either "translate" one myth into another, or analyse inverted structures in a single story. Carroll brings out the paradox of the Cain and Abel story quite well. Abel's sacrifice, although accepted by God, leads to death. Cain's (human?) sacrifice, even though it is rejected, does not lead to the fratricide's deserved death. Instead of giving access to divine blessing, health, prosperity, and life, sacrifice may also lead to death.

Leach uses two structural models to understand certain aspects of OT sacrifice. His first model concerns space. Our world, God's world, and a zone in which they overlap are symbolized in the various areas of the desert sanctuary or the Temple. The holy of holies belongs entirely to God's world, the courtyard to which laymen were admitted belongs to our world, and between the "lay" courtyard and the holy of holies is the overlapping zone – the area containing the altars of incense and burnt offerings. Leach's second model draws from the concept of *rite de passage*. The initiate is first ritually separated from society and exists outside society for a short period of social timelessness. After this lapse of time he is restored to society, but now in a new role.

Leach's description of the priestly consecration of Aaron and his sons (Lev. 8) fits well into the *rite de passage* model. Aaron and his sons are separated from the rest of the people by various rites which include the putting of sacrificial blood on their right ear, right thumb and right big toe. Then follows a period of seven days when Aaron and his sons are not to leave the sacred area. This is the period of social timelessness. As was seen by Douglas Davies, the *rite de passage* model also works well for the rehabilitation of the "leper" who has been cured. In this case the "leper" starts from being outside society. Initial rites bring him into a period of social timelessness lasting seven days. On the eighth day he is restored to full membership in society. At this stage the ritual includes the same putting of blood and oil on the right ear, right thumb, and right big toe.

Both Leach and Davies discuss the ritual of the Day of Atonement (Lev. 16) to which Frazer had devoted an entire volume of his *Golden Bough* and which continues to attract the attention of anthropologists.[21] Davies bases his interpretation on the idea of different areas of holiness: beginning with the holy of holies (as the most sacred part), passing through the camp (the area of ordered social relationships) to "outside the camp", the place of disorder. As the scapegoat passes progressively from the sphere of the divine to an area outside ordered relationships, it bears the iniquities of the congregation symbolically. This analysis fits the evidence better than Leach's *rite de passage* model. In the words of Rogerson, this model is

> unconvincing because the ritual says nothing about the period of social timelessness elsewhere essential to this model, and it is not clear to me who or what is to be changing its status. Leach seems to me to exaggerate in describing the scapegoat sequence as the "exact converse of the Aaron sequence".[22]

Using models, according to Rogerson, can be misleading. It may distort the evidence instead of being helpful. In this vein critics have argued that in reducing a literary work to a model, structuralism dislocates the author's intended meaning and eventually obliterates the actual text. Models and structures then are accorded a higher status than what is being analysed. On the other hand, it can be asked whether understanding is at all possible without reducing untidy evidence to models, structures, concepts, ideal types or the like.

For Leach, such models do not represent the eternal architecture of the human mind. They are partly patterns of aesthetic perception, partly "local, functionally determined, attributes of particular individuals or of particular cultural groups".[23] He frankly tells us that

Structuralist analyses do not yield solutions which are "right" or "wrong"; they demonstrate the existence of partial patterns. This provokes us to ask: is this significant or trivial? Further analysis will then reveal a more elaborate or perhaps a rather different pattern, and we are faced with the same question as before: does this give us "insight" or does it not? There is no end point at which the analyst can say: "There, I understand it all." At best he can simply feel that he understands rather more than when he started out.[24]

In this unique declaration of modesty Leach admits that structural analysis can be neither verified nor disproved. It is an art rather than a science. Its validity rests on intuition and the aesthetic satisfaction derived from recognizing or playing with "patterns".

On the other hand, Leach can be quite immoderate in his claims.[25] He tells the biblical student to reject the useless endeavours of comparative ethnography and to forget the purportedly historical framework in which the Bible stories are set. Instead, we should embrace the structural analysis of the Bible as an undifferentiated collection of "sacred tales". Although not many biblical scholars would endorse this radical view, here is a real problem. Historians and sociologists are inclined to exploit any biblical text in order to reconstruct Israel's social, religious, or political institutions. They might even use comparative ethnography to supplement their sources or help resolve confusion. In this context, literature is understood as a social phenomenon that cannot help echoing situations of normal life as well as historical events.

Other experts on the Old Testament have felt that literature must primarily be read as literature. They believe that the task of historical reconstruction from literary texts is problematic and perhaps should be abandoned. Since literature is a world complete in itself the historian simply asks the wrong questions. Literature must be approached as literature not as something else; therefore it can be structurally analysed. This collection of essays may help student and specialist alike to ponder such problems, and to appreciate the contributions of scholars devoted to comparative ethnography, the study of systems of classification, and structuralism.

The Anthropological Approach:
Today and Tomorrow

By selecting papers that elucidate individual biblical passages or themes, we have tried to represent fairly the varieties of anthropological approaches. We have not been able, however, to cover all the areas of biblical studies to which significant anthropological contributions have been made. Nor was it possible to indicate in which direction scholarship is likely to move and where good results are to be expected. It is to these questions that we will now turn.

When anthropologists write about a people they traditionally concentrate on their social, legal, economic and religious institutions to show what life is like in that society. One could say that to write such an account is the anthropologist's basic task. Depending on a historical reading of the Bible and some archaeological evidence, the eminent French Dominican scholar Roland de Vaux wrote such a work in the 1950s. Its English translation is called *Ancient Israel: Its Life and Institutions.*[26] This excellent book was rightly acclaimed as one of the finest contributions to biblical studies ever made. Although de Vaux's text retains its value, some scholars have pushed beyond de Vaux's ideas. Robert Wilson's paper on the mechanisms of judicial authority or Niels-Erik Andreasen's essay on the role of the Queen Mother[27] serve as significant revisions that use the anthropological approach. This is not to say that a revision of de Vaux's book is a task easy to accomplish. Many studies have yet to be written. For instance, there are valuable papers on various aspects of the Israelite kinship system,[28] but a comprehensive work on this subject is still missing.

There is no lack of recent and well-informed textbooks on ancient Israelite history. Written in the tradition of nineteenth-century historiography, these concentrate on political events and often do nothing else than paraphrase the few biblical and extrabiblical sources we have. Social and religious developments are given less attention, and a social–scientific analysis is not generally attempted. Anthropological models are rarely used to describe the formation of the Israelite state and the emergence of social classes. No doubt the day will come when the history of Israel will be rewritten in the light of the anthropological debate on the character of pre-state Israel, the formation of the monarchy, and similar discussions on other periods of biblical history. Norman Gottwald, James Flanagan, Robert Wilson, Frank Crüsemann, and Niels Peter Lemche

14

have made significant contributions to this debate.[29] There seems to be a vague consensus that the older view of a well-organized tribal league has to be abandoned or modified in the light of the more adequate model of a "society without rulers", known, for example, from the African Nuer referred to earlier in this introduction. Later periods of Israelite history have not received very much attention yet. There are, however, T. D. Proffitt's interesting paper on Moses as the prophet of a third-world-style millenarian or revitalization movement, D. Jobling's structuralist discussion of Transjordan as a "marginal territory" in Israelite geography, and H. G. Kippenberg's study on resistance against foreign rule in post-exilic Judaism.[30]

The scholar's encounter with biblical texts will no doubt continue to be influenced and shaped by anthropological knowledge and methods. Although structuralism may by now have lost some of its initial fascination, we can still expect significant contributions from its practitioners. A good example is Michael Carroll's paper on the stories of Esther, Judith, and Susanna.[31] Structuralism, however, is not the only method anthropology has to offer. Biblical scholars who rely on the established ways of form criticism and genre analysis often find themselves on the slippery ground of speculation when they postulate or reconstruct "earlier stages" of texts that were once in the oral mode. As is generally assumed, the original setting of songs, prayers, and tales was not literary, but oral. Some scholars have tried to explore the relevance of what anthropologists have found out about "oral literature", and their approach is very promising indeed. It may suffice to refer to Erhard Gerstenberger's *Der bittende Mensch* (a study that argues for a ritual setting of the psalms of individual complaint), Beat Zuber's *Vier Studien zu den Ursprüngen Israels* (which includes a valuable chapter on oral tradition and transmission in early Israel), and Burke Long's seminal paper on recent field studies in oral literature and their bearing on OT criticism.[32]

In the burgeoning, young field of anthropological study of the Bible methodological considerations are as important and inevitable as they are controversial. John Rogerson, Shemaryahu Talmon and myself[33] have warned of all-too-quick cross-cultural comparison and the not infrequently encountered use of outdated or problematic anthropological categories. While biblical scholars have to be careful not to rely on views of "survivals" or "magic" that have long been abandoned, anthropologists should be equally cautious in their use of scholarly and not-so-scholarly literature on biblical matters.

15

Many of them are handicapped by not knowing Hebrew, although the value of linguistic competence should not be exaggerated. Linguistic competence cannot compensate for anthropological ignorance. Robert Wilson has tried to establish some guidelines for the use of anthropology in biblical studies. He asserts, for instance, that "the most useful comparative material will come from studies dealing with the totality of a single society or with the social function of a phenomenon within several societies".[34] Crüsemann, on the other hand, insists that it may be safer and more rewarding not to use eclectic anthropological evidence from individual societies, but rather to rely on sophisticated theory that has been thoroughly tested in many cultures.[35] He would be more happy with anthropological studies that deal "with the social function of a phenomenon within several societies". Which would be more helpful, to compare individual extrabiblical prophets with those of the Bible, or to establish a general, cross-cultural theory of prophetic figures and their functions?[36] This is the kind of question that will no doubt provoke further discussion.

Closely related to the methodological issue is the debate about what is loosely termed "Hebrew thought". It is often assumed that the mind of the ancient Israelites is different from ours. As can be seen in Rogerson's paper, this assumption can severely distort the evidence by the use of doubtful concepts. On the other hand, there is no doubt that the Hebrew mind *can be* different from ours. But when precisely are the ancient Israelites like ourselves, and when aren't they? A significant contribution to this problem discusses the supposed power of words in Hebrew thought.[37] There is, however, much to be done in this field. Certain assumptions about the nature of prophetic symbolic acts as well as Klaus Koch's views of the act–consequence relationship have hardly begun to be evaluated critically.[38]

We have also to consider in what way the culture and religion – and thus the mind – of the Israelites is different from that of their ancient neighbours. An earlier debate about the supposedly unique Hebrew sense of "linear time" and history has hardly produced any significant results.[39] More promising is the anthropological study of the way in which Israelite culture *interacted* with neighbouring cultures. Many scholars agree that the ancient Israelites, apart from sharing certain common views, have extensively borrowed from other ancient cultures. Egyptian wisdom literature was adapted, Zoroastrian ideas of monotheism and resurrection assimilated, a hellenistic goddess, Isis, shaped the theology of the strictly monotheistic Book of Wisdom. Can anthropology help us to understand these instances of cultural contact? Kloppenborg, in a study on the Book of Wisdom, has referred to Lévi-Strauss' paper on "Relations of Symmetry between Rituals and Myths of Neighboring Peoples".[40] Lévi-Strauss proposes to look at neighbouring cultures as systems characterized by the sometimes conflicting wishes to maintain distinctive identity and to communicate with others. In the situation of cultural peace, neighbours must be "close enough to be friends and not far enough away to be enemies". It is to be hoped that professional anthropologists as specialists for "other cultures" join in such debates and help us to understand the Hebrew mind and mentality.

I venture to predict that what may now look like the fringe activity of a few anthropologists interested in the Bible and biblical scholars dissatisfied with more traditional ways of exegesis will develop into a recognized, established approach. Anthropologists who continue their interest in the OT will no doubt pay more attention to results of biblical scholarship. Some biblical scholars, on the other hand, will take anthropology as their guiding and inspiring model of research and explanation. What biblical scholars need are not only more answers, but also more questions. For them, anthropology would provide the questions to be asked, indicate important fields of research, offer material for cautious comparison, and be a centre for generalization and theory. Eventually, this may involve a major change in the nature of biblical studies. "Anthropology might serve to widen horizons for biblical scholars", explained Gillian Feeley-Harnik in her Centennial Address to the Society of Biblical Literature (1980),

> provided they are willing to admit ethnography into their domain, that is, to become students of comparative religion with a focus on the Bible and related material, as opposed simply to raiding the anthropological camp while leaving the "savage" safely behind.[41]

Biblical scholars as well as students will need to acquire some anthropological experience, if only by admitting other kinds of books to their shelves.

NOTES

The author acknowledges the editorial help of Dr Colleen McDannell, Philadelphia.

1 E. E. Evans-Pritchard, *Witchcraft, Oracles, and Magic among the Azande.* Abridged edn. (Oxford: Clarendon Press, 1976) 245.

Bernhard Lang

2 E. E. Evans-Pritchard, *Nuer Religion* (Oxford: OUP, 1956) vii.

3 One example may suffice: P. Walcot, *Greek Peasants, Ancient and Modern* (Manchester: Manchester University Press, 1970).

4 M. J. Field, *Angels and Ministers of Grace. An Ethno-Psychiatrist's Contribution to Biblical Criticism* (New York: Hill & Wang, 1972) xi.

5 H. Staden, *Warhaftig Historia und beschreibung eyner Landschafft der Wilden, Nacketen, Grimmigen, Menschenfressen Leuthen* (Frankfurt: Wüsten, 1927; facsimile of 1557 edn); the relevant passage is in part 2, ch. 23; M. de Montaigne, *Essays*. ET J. Florio, vol. 2 (London: Dent, 1910) 291.

6 Such eighteenth- and nineteenth-century compilations were published by Th. Harmer, S. Burder, W. Ward, and E. F. K. Rosenmüller. Recent and more sophisticated examples are R. Patai, *Sex and Family in the Bible and the Middle East* (Garden City, N.Y.: Doubleday, 1959); J. Morgenstern, *Rites of Birth, Marriage, Death and Kindred Occasions among the Semites* (Cincinnati: Hebrew Union College, 1966).

7 In the third letter, first published in 1780. The relevant passage is in J. G. Herder, *Sämmtliche Werke*, ed. B. Suphan, vol. 10 (Berlin: Weidmann, 1879) 38.

8 W. Robertson Smith, *Lectures on the Religion of the Semites*, 3rd edn 1927 (New York: KTAV, 1969; reprint).

9 "The use of keeping festivals is plain. Man derives benefit from such assemblies; the emotions produced renew the attachment to religion; they lead to friendly and social intercourse among the people." M. Maimonides, *The Guide for the Perplexed*, ET M. Friedländer (New York: Dover Publications, 1956) 366.

10 J. G. Frazer, *Folk-Lore in the Old Testament* (London: Macmillan, 1918), vol. 1, 45–77.

11 Cf. also: A. E. Jensen, "Beziehungen zwischen dem Alten Testament und der nilotischen Kultur in Afrika", in *Culture in History*, ed. S. Diamond (New York: Columbia Univ. Press, 1960) 449–66; E. A. McFall, *Approaching the Nuer of Africa through the Old Testament* (South Pasadena, Ca.: William Carey Library, 1970).

12 For recent discussions of the "corporate personality" concept see the survey of Gene M. Tucker in H. Wheeler Robinson, *Corporate Personality in Ancient Israel*, rev. edn (Philadelphia: Fortress, 1980) 7–13. Recently, a German author has based his psychoanalytical reading of biblical texts on "corporate personality understood not as a social, but a psychological phenomenon": Eugen Drewermann, *Tiefenpsychologie und Exegese*, vol. 1 (Olten: Walter Verlag, 1984) 271–98.

13 Cf. Jeremiah's smashing of a pot which symbolizes Jerusalem's impending destruction (Jer. 19). The Lévy-Bruhlian view is advocated, for instance, by H. W. Robinson, "Prophetic Symbolism", in *Old Testament Essays: Papers Read before the Society for Old Testament Studies at its 18th Meeting* (London: Griffin, 1927) 1–17. For a critique see Bernhard Lang, *Monotheism and the Prophetic Minority* (Sheffield: Almond Press, 1983) 88f.

14 Mary Douglas, *Implicit Meanings* (London: Routledge & Kegan Paul, 1975) 205.

15 M. Douglas, *Purity and Danger: An Analysis of the Concepts of Pollution and Taboo* (London: Routledge & Kegan Paul, 2nd edn 1969) 35f.

16 Douglas, *Purity and Danger*, 54; Frazer, *Folk-Lore in the Old Testament*, vol. 3, 160f.

17 Douglas, *Implicit Meanings*, 249–75 ("Deciphering a Meal") and 276–318 ("Self-Evidence").

18 Cf. also D. Sperber, "Pourquoi les animaux parfaits, les hybrides et les monstres sont-ils bons à penser symboliquement?", *L'Homme* 15 (1975) 5–34; G. J. Wenham, *The Book of Leviticus* (Grand Rapids, Mich.: Eerdmans, 1979) 164–85; E. Hunn, "The Abominations of Leviticus Revisited", in *Classifications in their Social Context*, ed. R. F. Ellen, D. Reason (London: Academic Press, 1979) 103–16; R. Alter, "A New Theory of Kashrut", *Commentary* 68/August (1979) 46–52; S. O. Murray, "Fuzzy Sets and Abominations", *Man* 18 (1983) 396–9.

19 In *Transactions of the New York Academy of Science*, 2nd series, vol. 23 (1961) 386–96.

20 E. R. Leach, *Genesis as Myth and Other Essays* (London: Cape, 1969); E. Leach, D. A. Aycock, *Structuralist Interpretations of Biblical Myth* (Cambridge: CUP, 1983). Cf. J. W. Rogerson, "Structural Anthropology and the Old Testament", *BSOAS* 33 (1970) 490–500; R. C. Culley, "Some Comments on Structural Analysis and Biblical Studies", in *Congress Volume Uppsala 1971* (VTSup 22; Leiden: Brill, 1972) 129–42; M. P. Carroll, "Leach, Genesis, and Structural Analysis", *AE* 4 (1977) 633–77 [partly reprinted in this volume as ch. 8].

21 J. G. Frazer, *The Golden Bough*, 3rd edn part 6: The Scapegoat (London: Macmillan, 1913) esp. 108–228.

22 J. W. Rogerson, "Sacrifice in the Old Testament", in *Sacrifice*, ed. M. F. C. Bourdillon, M. Fortes (London: Academic Press, 1980) 45–59, see p. 55.

23 E. R. Leach, *Lévi-Strauss*, rev. edn (Glasgow: W. Collins, 1974) 113.

24 Leach, *Structuralist Interpretations*, 4–5.

25 Leach, *Structuralist Interpretations*, 19–20, 29.

26 R. de Vaux, *Ancient Israel: Its Life and Institutions* (New York: McGraw-Hill, 1961).

27 R. R. Wilson, "Enforcing the Covenant: The Mechanism of Judicial Authority in Early Israel", in *The Quest for the Kingdom of God. Studies in Honor of G. E. Mendenhall*, ed. H. B. Huffmon *et al.* (Winona Lake, Ind.: Eisenbrauns, 1983) 59–75; N.-E. A. Andreasen, "The Role of the Queen Mother in Israelite Society", *CBQ* 45 (1983) 179–94.

28 T. J. Prewitt, "Kinship Structures and the Genesis Genealogies", *JNES* 40 (1981) 87–98; R. A. Oden, "Jacob as Father, Husband, and Nephew: Kinship Studies and the Patriarchal Narratives", *JBL* 102 (1983) 189–205.

29 N. K. Gottwald, *The Tribes of Yahweh: A Sociology of the Religion of Liberated Israel, 1250–1050 B.C.E.*(Maryknoll, N.Y.: Orbis, 1979); J. Flanagan, "Chiefs in Israel", *JSOT* 20 (1981) 47–73; R. R. Wilson, *Sociological Approaches to the Old Testament* (Philadelphia: Fortress, 1984) 30–53; F. Crüsemann, *Der*

Widerstand gegen das Königtum (WMANT 49; Neukirchen: Neukirchener Verlag, 1978) 195–222; N. P. Lemche, *Early Israel: Anthropological and Historical Studies on the Israelite Society before the Monarchy* (Leiden: Brill, 1985).

30 T. D. Proffitt, "Moses and Anthropology: A New View of the Exodus", *JETS* 27 (1984) 19–25; H. G. Kippenberg, *Religion und Klassenbildung im antiken Judäa* (SUNT 14; Göttingen: Vandenhoeck & Ruprecht, 2nd edn 1982); D. Jobling, "Levi-Strauss and the Structural Analysis of the Hebrew Bible", in *Anthropology and the Study of Religion*, ed. R. L. Moore *et al.* (Chicago: Center for the Scientific Study of Religion, 1984) 192–211.

31 M. P. Carroll, "Myth, Methodology and Transformation in the Old Testament: The Stories of Esther, Judith, and Susanna", *SR* 12 (1983) 301–12.

32 E. S. Gerstenberger, *Der bittende Mensch: Bittritual und Klagelied des Einzelnen im Alten Testament* (WMANT 51; Neukirchen: Neukirchener Verlag, 1980); B. O. Long, "Recent Field Studies in Oral Literature and their Bearing on OT Criticism". *VT* 26 (1976) 187–98; B. Zuber, *Vier Studien zu den Ursprüngen Israels* (Fribourg: Universitätsverlag, 1976).

33 J. W. Rogerson, *Anthropology and the Old Testament* (Oxford: Blackwell, 1978); S. Talmon, "The Comparative Method in Biblical Interpretation. Principles and Problems", in *Congress Volume Göttingen 1977* (VTSup 29; Leiden: Brill, 1978) 320–56; B. Lang, "Non-Semitic Deluge Stories and the Book of Genesis", *Anthropos* 80 (1985).

34 R. R. Wilson, *Prophecy and Society in Ancient Israel* (Philadelphia: Fortress, 1980) 15.

35 Crüsemann, *Der Widerstand gegen das Königtum*, 200.

36 Cf. V. E. Bonnell, "The Uses of Theory, Concepts and Comparison in Historical Sociology", *CSSH* 22 (1980) 156–73.

37 A. C. Thiselton, "The Supposed Power of Words in the Biblical Writings", *JTS* 25 (1974) 283–99.

38 C.-A. Keller, "Zum sog. Vergeltungsglauben im Proverbienbuch", in *Beiträge zur alttestamentlichen Theologie*, ed. H. Donner *et al.* (Göttingen: Vandenhoeck & Ruprecht, 1977) 223–38; J. Barton, "Natural Law and Poetic Justice in the Old Testament", *JTS* 30 (1979) 1–14; R. L. Hubbard, "Is the *Tatsphäre* Always a Sphere?", *JETS* 25 (1982) 257–62. Cf. above, note 13.

39 Cf. J. Barr, *Biblical Words for Time*, 2nd edn (London: SCM, 1969).

40 J. S. Kloppenborg, "Isis and Sophia in the Book of Wisdom", *HTR* 75 (1982) 57–84, p. 82ff.; cf. C. Lévi-Strauss, "Relations of Symmetry between Rituals and Myths of Neighboring Peoples", in *Structural Anthropology*, vol. 2 (New York: Basic Books, 1976) 238–56.

41 G. Feeley-Harnik, "Is Historical Anthropology Possible?", in *Humanizing America's Iconic Book*, ed. G. M. Tucker, D. A. Knight (Chico, Ca.: Scholars Press, 1982) 95–126, see p. 99.

1

Enslavement and the
Early Hebrew Lineage System

An Explanation of
Genesis 47:29–31; 48:1–16[*]

FRANZ STEINER

In[1] his recent *Studies in Biblical Law*, David Daube has analysed the story of Joseph in order to find the concomitant legal conceptions of the early Hebrews: his main reference was to the first part of the story.[2] Here I want to examine what I regard as the climax of the biblical narrative.

If, as is often done, we consider the story of Joseph simply as a tale, the consummate artistry with which the narrative is unfolded imposes as the climax the meeting of Joseph and his brothers in Egypt. If, however, we consider the Joseph story basically as a description of a man whose kinship bonds were severed by his sale into slavery and of his later relations to his kinship group, the climax is revealed in the passages which I want to examine here. Some years' study of servile institutions and their structural ramifications in simpler societies[3] have enabled me to elucidate certain features of the biblical narrative which before seemed difficult.

Among the relevant verses (Gen. 47:29–31; 48:1–16), the following are the ones of chief interest:

> Gen. 47:29   And the time drew nigh that Israel must die; and he called his son Joseph, and said unto him, If now I have found grace in thy sight, put, I pray thee, thy hand under my thigh, and deal kindly and truly with me; bury me not, I pray thee, in Egypt.
>
> 47:31   And he said, Swear unto me. And he sware unto him. And Israel [i.e., Jacob] bowed himself upon the bed's head.

*First published in *Man* 54 (1954) 73–5.

48:5 And now thy two sons, Ephraim and Manasseh, which were born
unto thee in the land of Egypt before I came unto thee into Egypt, are
mine; as Reuben and Simeon, they shall be mine.
48:6 And thy issue, which thou begettest after them, shall be thine
and shall be called after the name of their brethren in their inheritance.

In the first place, it is surprising to find Jacob addressing his son
in this deferential manner. Interpetations which account for this by
Joseph's exalted position in Egypt do not take cognisance of the
father–son relationship in the patriarchal society of the Hebrews.

The second difficulty is the oath. To "put the hand under the
thigh" has been interpreted by the leading commentators (e.g.
Rashi)[4] as touching the genitals, and this act is quite inconsistent
with the fundamental family taboo of the Hebrews. The only other
instance of putting one's hand under a person's thigh while making
a vow does not refer to such a contact between near kinsmen, let
alone between a son and his progenitor; it is the description of the
oath of Abraham's servant Eliezer (Gen. 24:2).

The notion that, as Franz Delitzsch puts it, "Jacob desires Joseph
to put his hand under his thigh, and thus to assure him on the
ground of the covenant of circumcision made with Abraham, the
actual proof of faithful love ..."[5] had to be discarded after
Pedersen's study of the oath among the Semites. Pedersen compares
the biblical procedure with similar customs found among the Arabs
who, however, swear by their own, not by the other person's,
genitals. According to Pedersen, in the Arab formula, the male
genitals signify the children, and, what is more, the whole kin.
Among the Arabs it is thus "an oath by that kin from which (the
person who swears) will be severed if he violates his vow".[6] This
Arab procedure would be nonsensical if it were used in an agreement
between persons deeply interested in the well-being of the identical
group of people. To this must be added the inconsistency we have
already mentioned: the severe Hebrew family taboo (Gen. 9:21–5;
Lev. 18:6–18).

There seems to be only one answer: that Joseph, because of his
sale into slavery, is legally no longer Jacob's son. This selling is a
renunciation of family solidarity with and responsibility for Joseph,
and although the sale took place without the father's knowledge,
it must affect the father as it does all other kinsmen. This would
explain Jacob's deferential address: as this is a formal occasion and
binding promises are to be given, the words exchanged between the

two persons must, in a formal manner, exactly correspond to their actual social relationship.

This explanation also throws some light on the third point: the sons of Joseph are to be received as future progenitors and *patres* of the "tribes" into what Professors Evans-Pritchard and M. Fortes call the "maximal lineage".[7] No such attention is given to the other grandchildren of Jacob. There are no grounds for regarding this as a mark of deference to or as an indemnification of Joseph; Joseph expresses no gratitude for having been preferred to his brothers.

Holzinger is one of the many who have dealt with the passage according to the rules of "Higher Criticism". He distinguishes two different narratives which have been combined: in the one narrative Joseph's sons are blessed, but not Joseph himself; in the other narrative, Jacob, after going through a rite of adoption by having the lads sit on his knees, returns them to Joseph, blessing him, "but his words shift to the children very quickly".[8]

It is not within the power of Joseph's former kinship group to take him back. He has become a freeman in Egypt, but this does not make him a member of his family again. On the contrary, having been freed in Egypt he then became attached to the court of the king, and in that capacity he is part of the Egyptian social structure.

In most societies a slave's manumission makes him a member or an affiliated member (client) of the former master's family. In fact, in ancient Mesopotamia, adoption seems to have been one of the chief forms of enfranchisement. Adoption or clientage does not reinstate the former slave into his previous kinship structure.[9] Much depends on the mode of enslavement. We know of most simpler societies that aliens who had been enslaved against the will of their smallest solidarity group, e.g. as prisoners of war, tend to run away; a man sold by his family rarely does so.

Perhaps quite a different case in an entirely different social setting may help to explain further the nature of this kinship obligation in the enslavement complex.

In her description of the institutions of the North-west American Tsimshian, Viola E. Garfield mentions a case of enslavement. A chief wanted "to humble a rich and powerful lineage in his tribe, a lineage of which he was jealous". He asked for one of their women in marriage, and sold her after the wedding to a neighbouring chief. Her relatives bought her free, but could not refuse the influential chief when he asked for her again. Once more she was sold and redeemed, and yet a third time was asked in marriage by the same chief. By then the family had been considerably impoverished, and when they gave the woman away, they made public in the appropriate manner, that they were not going to ransom her any more. "So far as they were concerned she was dead." Her name was no more mentioned by her people, and she died a slave.[10]

This declaration as dead means the formal renunciation of all kinship obligations and this is implied in every sale into slavery by a person's kinship group – in cases where slavery is institutionalized, and if the "sale" is not merely a selling into debtor slavery. The latter is a very common institution of African and Malaysian societies. There, the fact that the party selling retains the right to redeem the person who is sold, means that kinship obligations are acknowledged.

The sociological and historical significance of this part of the Joseph story is twofold. The legal conceptions underlying it are different from the slave law of Exodus, Deuteronomy and Leviticus, which correspond to the slave laws of the Mesopotamian cultures. Both kinds of society, differ as they may amongst themselves, are no longer tribal societies in the strict sense. Both kinds of society distinguish between two categories of slaves: nationals and enslaved aliens. The later biblical law conceives of the enslaved male nationals as temporary slaves. The point of interest is not so much the possibility of automatic release after the fixed number of years (Exod. 21:2), but the unbroken kinship ties with and obligations towards the enslaved which make them "nationals". In this lies the chief difference between alien and national slaves, not in the participation in the activities of the ritual community. In this latter respect, as Isaac Mendelsohn has recently pointed out,[11] the two groups are hardly distinguishable.

I suggest that the Joseph story goes a long way in explaining the evolution which led to the later legal customs.

Moreover, these passages describe to us minutely a lineage system working in a way we would not expect among the Semites. The reason is that we have tended to investigate the kinship organization of the Semites more in terms of family units than in terms of lineages. The splitting off and the reabsorption of the minimal lineage remind us of phases in the growth of African kinship groups, as described by Evans-Pritchard and Fortes.

NOTES

1 The bibliographical references, lacking in the manuscript, have been supplied by Laura Bohannan, and revised by B. Lang.

2 David Daube, *Studies in Biblical Law* (Cambridge: CUP, 1947) 3–15.

3 Franz Steiner, *Comparative Study of Servile Institutions* (unpublished PhD thesis, Oxford).

4 See Rashi on Gen. 24:2.

5 Franz Delitzsch, *A New Commentary on Genesis*, ET S. Taylor (Edinburgh: T. & T. Clark, 1888) vol. 2, 355.

6 Johs. Pedersen, *Der Eid bei den Semiten* (Strasbourg: K. J. Trübner, 1914) 150f.

7 *African Political Systems*, ed. Meyer Fortes and Edward E. Evans-Pritchard (London: OUP, 1940).

8 H. Holzinger, *Genesis*. Kurzer Hand-Commentar zum Alten Testament (Freiburg: J. C. B. Mohr, 1898) 253.

9 Isaac Mendelsohn, *Slavery in the Ancient Near East* (New York: OUP, 1949) 1–33; also Edith J. Simcox, *Primitive Civilisations* (London: S. Sonnenschein, 1894) passim.

10 Viola E. Garfield, "Tsimshian Clan and Society". *Univ. of Washington Publications in Anthropology*, vol. 7, no. 3 (Seattle, 1939) 167–340; see p. 272.

11 Mendelsohn, *Slavery in the Ancient Near East*, 37–74.

2

*The Sin of Cain**

ISAAC SCHAPERA

The third chapter of Frazer's *Folk-Lore in the Old Testament* is entitled "The Mark of Cain".[1] It will be remembered that, after Cain had killed his younger brother Abel, God drove him away and condemned him to be a "fugitive and wanderer". And when Cain protested at the greatness of his punishment, saying that whoever found him would slay him, God replied: "Not so! If any one slays Cain, vengeance shall be taken on him sevenfold." "And", the narrative continues, "the Lord put a mark on Cain, lest any who came upon him should kill him" (Gen. 4:8-15).

Like many an earlier commentator, Frazer was particularly interested in the nature of the "mark" by which Cain was protected. He reviews briefly, and discards, the varying explanations of such men as Robertson Smith and Stade, and then, ignoring Driver's opinion that in this connection "it is idle to speculate", since what the mark was "is not stated",[2] he draws upon comparative ethnography for an explanation of his own. "The mark of Cain", he concludes after a survey of analogous instances, "may have been a mode of protecting a homicide against his victim's ghost, either by disguising him or by rendering him formidable and repulsive."[3]

> This explanation [he continues] has the advantage of relieving the biblical narrative from a manifest absurdity. For on the usual interpretation God affixed the mark of Cain in order to save him from human assailants, apparently forgetting that there was nobody to assail him, since the earth was as yet inhabited only by the murderer himself and his parents. Hence by assuming that the foe of whom the first murderer went in fear was a ghost instead of a living man, we avoid the irreverence of imputing to the deity a grave lapse of memory little in keeping with the divine omniscience. Here again, therefore, the comparative method approves itself a powerful *advocatus Dei* [apologist for God].[4]

*First published in *JRAI* 85 (1955) 33–43. In the interest of brevity the notes have been slightly abridged.

It is pleasantly ironic to find Frazer rallying to the support of a deity whom his own writings, notably *The Golden Bough*, are sometimes said to have done much to discredit. But in his zeal he seems to have overlooked one possible implication of his theory: if we accept it, we must assume also that God's protection of Cain went so far as to include the threat of retaliation against the ghost of Abel should the latter seek vengeance.

Nor do I see the same difficulty as he and others in determining who there was to avenge the death of Abel. In early biblical times, a father had power of life and death over his children;[5] and in the scene where Reuben offers his two sons to Jacob as a pledge for the safe return of Benjamin from Egypt, the patriarch is explicitly invited to slay the youths should his favourite not be brought back to him (Gen. 42:37). We are told also that when Athaliah, mother of Ahaziah, learned of her son's assassination, "she arose and destroyed all the royal family of the house of Judah", i.e. all the other sons of her husband (2 Chron. 22:10; 2 Kgs 11:1). Presumably, therefore, it would have been both possible and justifiable for Adam, or even Eve, to avenge Abel's murder had either been so inclined.

And this brings me to the topic that I wish to discuss here, a topic that does not seem to have received the attention it deserves. The OT is explicit and uncompromising in regard to murder. "You shall not kill", says the sixth commandment (Exod. 20:13). The penalty for infringement is always death. "Whoever strikes a man so that he dies shall be put to death", says the Book of the Covenant (Exod. 21:12); or, in the more familiar words of the Priestly Code, "Whoever sheds the blood of man, by man shall his blood be shed" (Gen. 9:6). And although after the conquest of Palestine cities of refuge were established to which accidental killers could flee, the law against deliberate homicide, of the kind committed by Cain, remained so precise that a murderer who had fled to such a city could be extradited and handed over for execution to "the avenger of blood" (Deut. 19:4–13).

Moreover, as just indicated, whenever a man was killed, his nearest kinsmen were expected to avenge him,[6] although after the establishment of the monarchy their right to do so became subject to the approval of the central authority (2 Sam. 14:4ff.). Several instances are recorded where vengeance was in fact taken. Thus, Gideon slew the two Midianite chiefs who had killed his brothers in battle (Judg. 8:18–21); Joab treacherously slew Abner for a similar injury, despite the safe conduct granted by David (2 Sam.

2:23; 3:26–30); Amaziah, after succeeding to the throne of Judah, "killed his servants who had slain the king his father" (2 Kgs 14:5); and the killing of Saul's sons and grandsons by the Gibeonites (2 Sam. 16:1–9) shows that if the original offender was no longer alive vengeance could be exercised even upon his descendants. This last example, incidentally, is a case in which the injured group appealed to the king, who then handed the responsible persons over to them for execution.

Why then, in the particular instance with which we are here concerned, should Cain's life have been spared, and the only penalty inflicted upon him be one of outlawry? In the wilderness, admittedly, he was at the mercy of whoever found him and, as he himself feared, might be slain with impunity; and it was specifically to protect him from this that God "put a mark" on him. But why was he outlawed in the first place, and not treated like any other murderer?

The question has little point if we accept the view of some modern scholars that the story of Cain and Abel symbolizes a conflict between pastoral and cultivating tribes. But if, following orthodox commentators, we take the story at face value (and, like Frazer, I am here interested not in its historicity, but in the kind of social system it portrays), we are, I think, justified in asking why Cain should have escaped the fate of the ordinary murderer.

Jewish folklore has it that the death penalty for murder was divinely instituted only after and because of Cain's deed, and that since he himself had not been instructed against shedding blood he was explicitly exempted from the punishment that would apply to future murderers.[7] Biblical commentators, whether Jewish or Christian, have tended to avoid the problem. They usually say that Cain's punishment was mitigated, either as an act of divine grace or (with less justification) because he was a repentant sinner, but they do not try to explain why that punishment should originally have taken the form that it did.

If I may for the moment indulge in paradox, I would suggest that Cain escaped the standard penalty because the person whom he had killed was his brother. And here it must be noted that in apparently none of the other instances of actual fratricide recorded in the OT did the killer meet with death at the hands of the rightful human avenger. Abimelech killed all his seventy brothers but one, and then governed Israel for several years before being killed while besieging Thebez (Judg. 9); Absalom, after killing Amnon, fled from home but was not pursued, and ultimately was recalled and forgiven by David (2 Sam. 13:14); Solomon, after killing Adonijah, ruled as king of Israel for many years and in the end died peacefully (2 Kgs 2:13–25; 12:43); and Jehoram, who not only killed all his brothers but reverted to paganism, was ultimately smitten by God with a painful and fatal disease (2 Chron. 21).

The situation revealed by the biblical laws and narratives may at this stage be summarized briefly. Murder is an offence whose prescribed penalty is death inflicted in retaliation by the victim's next of kin. Several instances are recorded in which such vengeance was duly carried out, even long after the murder itself. But in certain other instances, where the murderer and his victim were brothers, the *lex talionis* did not in fact operate; and of the men concerned only Abimelech and Jehoram, but not Cain, Absalom, or Solomon, are stated to have died violently by the will of God – and in the list of Jehoram's crimes, incidentally, apostasy takes precedence over fratricide (2 Chron. 21:12,13).

The biblical situation has many parallels. In some primitive societies, for example, a distinction is commonly made between the killing of a kinsman and the killing of an outsider. Most of the instances recorded relate to societies in which homicide is regarded, not as a crime, but as a tort against the victim's relatives (or, in Radcliffe-Brown's terminology, as a private and not as a public delict).

In such societies there are two main varieties of penalty for the offence.[8] The first is retaliation: a life for a life. This takes many forms, but the basic principle is that the victim's relatives are entitled and expected to avenge him, by killing either the murderer himself or someone else of the same kinship group. Good examples are provided by the Bushmen and Hottentots of South Africa, among whom vengeance is the only sanction employed when murderer and victim belong to different groups.[9]

The second type of penalty, which according to some writers is a later development made possible by the existence of recognized mediums of exchange, is the payment of compensation. This usually consists of livestock or some other commodity, although occasionally the victim is replaced by another person of the same sex and approximate age, or else his family are given a woman to bear them a substitute. When compensation is in kind, the murderer's relatives help him with the payment, which after receipt is divided among those of the victim. Vengeance and compensation sometimes occur together, as when the injured group has the option of choosing between them, or perhaps may exercise vengeance only if the murderer is caught soon after the act, but failing that must accept compensation. Such alternatives are found, for example, among the Nandi, Kikuyu, and Vugusu, of Kenya, and the Mesakin of the Nuba Hills in Kordofan.[10]

Now among the peoples just named (and I have chosen them because they exemplify what I wish to say), the customary sanctions are apparently not enforced against a man killing a member of his own kinship group. Sometimes he is not punished at all (e.g.. Bushmen, Hottentots, Nandi, Kikuyu, and Vugusu), or else the compensation payable is greatly reduced (e.g., some groups of Kikuyu, and occasionally among the Nandi). Let me illustrate this by two quotations. Wandres, our main authority on Hottentot law, says that vengeance for homicide is normally "a sacred duty"; but, he adds, in cases of fratricide "the parents may intervene to prevent further bloodshed, and so that they should not be deprived of a second son the culprit will be forgiven".[11] For the Bushmen, we have the following case-history recorded by the traveller Burchell who in 1811 encountered a small group of about twenty persons, headed by an old man, in the vicinity of what is now Griquatown:

> They related to us, without the least emotion, and with apparent indifference, a horrid occurrence which had lately taken place in their kraal. This old man had three sons, one of whom had been married several years to a woman by whom he had two children. One of the brothers had conceived a liking for the woman, and she on her part was not averse to change her husband; it was therefore agreed between them, that he should be put out of the way. This (I shudder in relating it) was accomplished by the atrocious demon beating out his brother's brains as he lay asleep. This inhuman act appears to have excited no feeling of horror in the horde: the pair were at this time living together contented, and, seemingly, undismayed by their own reflections on the nefarious deed they had committed. Conscience herself seemed to have neglected her duty, and bestial ignorance to have usurped her place. Instead of chasing him for ever out of their kraal, the father and the remaining brother allowed him to continue in their society on the same terms as if nothing of the kind had happened. I saw the murderer; he was a youth of apparently seventeen or eighteen years of age, and of not an unpleasing countenance.[12]

The Mesakin, again, distinguish two kinds of killing of kin: the killing of a fellow-clansman, and the killing of a closer relative, such as a brother. In the former event, nothing is done to the culprit, except that like all other homicides he must perform a purification ceremony to ward off supernatural punishment for his deed. But if a man kills his brother, the ceremony does not help, and unless he chooses to go into exile he will be afflicted with leprosy; his offence, as Nadel says, "is a sin rather than a crime".[13]

A somewhat analogous conception is described by Robertson Smith.[14] If a man kills a stranger, he says, "a blood-feud at once arises, and the slain man may be avenged by any member of his own group on any member of the group of the slayer. The dead man's kin make no effort to discover and punish the individual slayer; they hold his whole kin responsible for his act, and take vengeance on the first of them on whom they can lay hands." But if a man kills one of his own kin, he is either "put to death by his own people or he becomes an outlaw and must take refuge in an alien group". He has committed "an inexpiable offence, for which no compensation can be taken"; he has shed the blood of his people, and his "execution or banishment is a religious duty, for if it is not performed the anger of the deity rests on the whole kin; therefore it is important to discover and punish the criminal himself."

Among the Bedouin of the Sinai Peninsula, on the other hand, retaliation is in most cases of homicide averted by paying a standard rate of compensation in camels; but, we are told, "if a man were to murder his brother, the amount of bloodmoney paid would depend entirely on what was agreed upon in the family"; and the father, if still alive, "might possibly induce the victim's next of kin [presumably his children] to accept a reduction for the sake of peace in the family".[15]

The various peoples to whom I have so far referred live either in small autonomous communities, or in segments lacking a common centralized authority with power to regulate vengeance or to enforce the payment of compensation. Sometimes, as for example among the Kikuyu and the Bedouin, there is formal machinery for arbitration between different groups, but in the last resort the injured group is itself responsible for obtaining satisfaction. Among peoples united under the rule of a single government whose functions include the administration of justice, homicide is still often regarded as a tort. But here there is an important difference in procedure. If the two groups concerned are unable to settle matters peacefully, by direct negotiation, the victim's relatives must sue in the tribal courts; should they take the law into their own hands, they are themselves guilty of an offence and liable to punishment.

This occurs, for example, among the North-eastern Sotho and the Southern Sotho of South Africa. Here vengeance for homicide is not permitted. The normal penalty is compensation; the standard rate, among both peoples, is ten head of cattle, although among the North-eastern Sotho a young woman may be given instead to bear a substitute for the dead person. Should the murderer's kin refuse to pay compensation, the tribal courts will enforce it, and among the Southern Sotho they will then usually also impose a fine. But, and here we get back to our main theme; no compensation at all is payable if murderer and victim belong to the same family, although among the North-eastern Sotho the culprit is sometimes expelled from his village.[16]

The examples that I have given, and many more of the same kind have been recorded,[17] show then that in some primitive societies the man who kills a kinsman does not meet the fate of the ordinary homicide; but he may be treated more leniently or even not penalized at all, or on the other hand he may be dealt with more severely (as among the Arabs) or suffer distinctive supernatural punishment (as among the Mesakin).

It has been suggested by some writers that the difference between the two categories of homicide is due to the belief that the murder of a kinsman is a particularly heinous offence, a sacrilege for which the normal sanctions are inadequate. Hence the murderer is either abandoned to the inevitable and relentless wrath of the gods, or, since he is a source of pollution, his relatives immediately get rid of him by execution or banishment. This, as we have seen, is the way in which Robertson Smith explains the Arab usages, and it also features prominently in the view developed by Mauss and other writers of the Durkheim school about the religious origins of penal law.[18]

But although many apt illustrations can be found (the well-known story of Oedipus is a case in point), the killing of a relative is by no means always held to be a sacrilege, or a source of special pollution. The concept certainly does not occur among any of the South African peoples that I have mentioned; the tribal histories of the Sotho, for example, like those of all other southern Bantu, record many instances of patricide and fratricide in royal families, with never a suggestion that such killings were in any way more reprehensible than the killing of an unrelated person.

Nor can we say that the biblical Hebrews regarded fratricide as an offence more atrocious or sinful than any other kind of murder. It is true that the shedding of human blood was held to pollute the ground, a feature specifically mentioned in the story of Cain (Gen. 4:10ff.), but the pollution resulted from bloodshed of any kind, and not only from the killing of a kinsman.[19] And when we remember that, apart from the instances of actual fratricide already mentioned, the Bible also records, in very prosaic language, how Esau planned to kill Jacob (Gen. 27:41) and how it was only through Reuben's intervention that Joseph was not killed by his other brothers (Gen. 38:18–22), we can hardly assume that this particular form of homicide was thought to entail either distinctive supernatural penalties or the murderer's execution or banishment by the whole of his kin.

Other writers have suggested that a fratricide is treated differently because in his case compensation is superfluous: since his relatives are normally expected to help him, there is little point in their insisting upon his making them a payment to which they themselves will have to contribute.[20] This explanation is obviously valid, if at all, only for societies in which compensation is one of the recognized ways of dealing with homicide. Nor is it applicable to the biblical situation since, with the dubious exception of the Gibeonites (2 Sam. 21:4), there is no record of compensation being sought or offered when one man kills another;[21] the Priestly Code, indeed, specifically prohibits it (Num. 35:31ff.).

A similar line of argument has sometimes been used to explain the immunity of fratricides in those societies where, as in ancient Israel, the normal penalty for homicide is blood vengeance. The group, it is suggested, has already been deprived of one member, and to kill the murderer as well would merely mean that it suffers a further loss. This, it will be recalled, is the explanation given for a father's intervening to prevent the taking of vengeance upon his fratricide son among the Hottentots.

But I doubt if even this covers all the instances recorded in the OT. When Cain was driven away, he was lost to his parents as effectively as if he too had been killed; we are told that David pined for the return of Absalom, yet took no steps to recall him until Joab intervened (2 Sam. 13:39; 14:1–28); and when Reuben pledged the lives of his two sons to Jacob as security for the safe return of Benjamin (Gen. 42:37), he does not seem to have been deterred by the prospect that if his mission failed the family would be still further depleted.

It is perhaps only in the scene where Rebekah sends Jacob away, having learned that Esau was planning to kill him, that the fear of double loss is stressed. "Why", said she, "should I be bereft of you both in one day?" (Gen. 27:45). One interpretation of her words is that she feared the loss of both her husband and her favourite son, since Esau was planning to kill Jacob as soon as Isaac had died. Most commentators, however, suggest that she was referring to the possibility of Esau's being killed in retaliation by the avenger of blood, or of his fleeing to escape that penalty.

And here we must notice another passage in the Bible, which, although the incident to which it refers is fictitious, indicates very clearly that the usual vengeance might indeed be exercised upon a man who had slain his brother. It occurs in the description of David's interview with the "wise woman of Tekoa", who was sent to him by Joab to induce him to recall Absalom. "I am a widow", she told the king, and continued:

> And your handmaid had two sons, and they quarrelled with one another in the field; there was no one to part them, and one struck the other and killed him. And now the whole family has risen against your handmaid, and they say, "Give up the man who struck his brother, that we may kill him for the life of his brother whom he slew"; and so they would destroy the heir also. Thus they would quench my coal which is left, and leave to my husband neither name nor remnant upon the face of the earth. (2 Sam. 14:5–7)

The story ends with David's undertaking to protect the surviving son from the "avenger of blood", whereupon the woman retorts that if he is willing to do that he should also forgive and recall his own son.

From this, and from the passages relating to Reuben and possibly Rebekah, we must conclude that there was actually no recognized legal discrimination between the killing of a relative and the killing of some other person. Can we in any way reconcile this with the immunity from blood vengeance recorded of such true fratricides as Cain, Abimelech, Absalom, Solomon, and Jehoram? The case of Absalom is particularly relevant in this context since it was contemporaneous with, and indeed provided the occasion for, the story invented by the woman of Tekoa: in that story, the next of kin are represented as seeking legitimate revenge, yet the sole purpose of its telling is to ensure that no such revenge will be taken on Absalom, and that, instead, he will be restored to the bosom of his family.

Here we may turn again for guidance to comparative ethnography. In many primitive societies every person belongs to an extended kinship group such as a lineage or a clan, and almost always his nearest neighbours include some of his fellow-members. In relation to the outside world, the members of such a group tend to constitute a single undifferentiated unit. They are held jointly responsible for an injury committed by any one of them, and reciprocally an injury against an individual is regarded as an injury against the group. Consequently, when a man is killed by an outsider, his group as a whole is affected and takes whatever action is appropriate, and not the murderer specifically but his kinsmen collectively must answer for the deed.

This accounts for some of the more common features of both blood vengeance and composition to which I have already referred; and the same point is made, it will be remembered, by Robertson Smith in his description of what happens in cases of homicide among the Arabs. It also explains why, for example, the Gibeonites were entitled to kill Saul's descendants in revenge for a wrong that he himself had done to them. It was only when the monarchy was well established in ancient Israel that the principle of collective responsibility began to disappear. We are told, as if it deserved special mention, that when Amaziah killed his father's assassins he did not also kill their children (2 Kgs 14:5ff.; 2 Chron. 25:3ff.); and the well-known injunction, "The fathers shall not be put to death for the children, nor shall the children be put to death for the fathers; every man shall be put to death for his own sin" (Deut. 24:16), belongs to one of the later legal codes.

Now, as we have already seen, in societies composed of autonomous local communities, or divided into segments not united under the rule of a single central authority, the killing of a man by someone of a different group often leads to feud or some similar state of hostility, unless and until compensation is paid or other satisfaction obtained. The less closely the two groups are connected, the larger is the number of people involved, and the more widespread and extensive the disturbance of social relations.

This has been admirably illustrated by Evans-Pritchard[22] in his discussion of feuds among the Nuer. When homicide occurs between separate tribal sections – and this usually happens in fights where several persons are killed – there is, he says, "little chance of an early settlement and, owing to distance, vengeance is not easily achieved, so that unsettled feuds accumulate". Moreover, it is not only the lineages which have taken a life or lost a member that are involved; "through common residence, local patriotism, and a network of kinship ties, the whole sections participate in the enmity that results, and the prosecution of the feuds may lead to further fighting between the communities concerned and to a multiplication of feuds between them." On the other hand, "when a man kills a near kinsman or close neighbour, the matter is quickly closed"; general opinion within the village "demands an early settlement, since it is obvious to everyone that were vengeance allowed corporate life would be impossible"; consequently, compensation, "often on a reduced scale", is "soon offered and accepted".

The relevant feature here is that when a man kills someone of his own group, no outsiders are involved; the people affected are all related to one another by ties of close kinship and common residence, and, since they have to live together, their primary concern is to restore peaceful relations as soon as possible, even if this means forgoing the usual full-scale retaliation.

It is significant, in this context, that even among such African peoples as the Sotho, who have well-established systems of central government, the head of every local kinship group is a judge of first instance for his people. Moreover, it is a recognized principle of tribal law that disputes among relatives are essentially their own concern; so long as no outsiders are involved, so long as there is no threat of general disturbance of the peace, they can deal with the matter as they wish. As the Tswana say, *Fa gare ga bana ba mpa ga go tsenwe*, "Outsiders should not intrude upon the affairs of the kin." It is only if the head of the group cannot settle a matter to the satisfaction of all concerned that it is taken to a higher court, and failing that even the chief himself cannot intervene.

This was strikingly illustrated during the course of a discussion that I once had about incest with the chief of the Ngwaketse and some of his advisers. They cited as an example a man who had married his paternal half-sister, and said that such a union was wrong and should not have taken place. When asked why he had not proceeded against the offenders, the chief replied simply that he could do nothing, as the marriage had not given rise to any dispute that would bring it to the official cognizance of his court; it was for the nearest relatives of the couple to complain if they were offended, and since they had not done so he was not entitled to interfere.[23] The same chief's father, incidentally, was once severely reprimanded by his headmen for personally searching huts where he thought liquor was being illegally concealed; it was their duty, they said, and not his, to see to the maintenance of law and order within their own groups.

This emphasis among the Tswana on the right of self-determination by the kinship group is reflected also by what sometimes happens when a man kills a near relative. Unlike other Sotho, the

Tswana treat homicide not as a tort that can be compounded, but as a crime, which is tried in the chief's court and punished with death, banishment, or a fine, according to the circumstances of the killing. The verdict is normally decided by the chief; but in several instances, where only kinsfolk were involved, the victim's nearest relatives were allowed to intervene.

In one such case, which occurred among the Kgatla about 1880, before the imposition of European rule, a man named Matshabe had cold-bloodedly shot and killed his father's brother's son; the victim's father was asked what punishment he wanted inflicted, and when he insisted on death, since he wished to avenge the loss of his only son, he was handed a loaded gun and told to execute the sentence himself, which he did. In another, which occurred among the neighbouring Kwena about 1870, a youth named Molefi had killed his elder brother; the chief proposed to inflict the death penalty, but the father successfully objected and himself contributed to the payment of the fine that was then substituted.[24] In 1926 there was another case of fratricide among the Kwena. The culprit, named Ramodisanyane, was tried by the Administration, and acquitted, since the killing was evidently accidental; but his relatives, including his own wife and children, refused to have him back, because (as they said) of his "murdering habits", and the chief, unwilling to be responsible for his safety, therefore ordered him to leave the tribe.

The cases just cited illustrate another feature, which is characteristic also of all the other South African peoples that I have mentioned. When a man injures someone else of his own group, the principle of undifferentiated collective responsibility ceases to apply; after all, the group has not only been injured, but has also offended, and it can hardly be expected to retaliate against its own members indiscriminately. This is especially true when culprit and victim belong to a minimal lineage or even to the same family, and where consequently only a few people are directly concerned. In such cases, only the culprit and his immediate dependants tend to be held responsible. If he has killed a brother, for example, his father and other brothers, or the sons of the dead brother, may take action against him and his children; but they will certainly not seek satisfaction by retaliating against another brother or cousin instead. The smaller the group, therefore, the more likelihood is there of the culprit's alone being held responsible – even to the extent, as we saw for the Kwena, of his own wife and children turning against him.

One consequence, I suggest, is that all this permits of much greater flexibility in dealing with internal offenders. Instead of being bound by the formal pattern that governs the relations of different groups, the members of the group concerned are relatively free to do whatever seems best to them. What action they do in fact take will in the last resort probably depend upon the particular circumstances of each case: the esteem in which the offender was previously held, his status in the group, the motives for his deed, the provocation he might have had, the degree of support he commands, the identity and popularity of his victim, etc.

Such factors are certainly of great significance among the Sotho in determining how a man's local relatives react to an offence that he commits against one of them. It must be realized that he lives in continuous and intimate association with them, works and relaxes with them, and usually helps them, as they help him, in the event of trouble with people of other groups. Hence, if they are on good terms with him, they are usually willing to claim nominal damages, or even to overlook his offence altogether; for example, unmarried youths are often advised to confine their love affairs to their own group, so that if they make a girl pregnant their family will not have to pay the full damages that unrelated people would normally demand. But if there is ill-feeling – and the close proximity in which they live inevitably breeds jealousies and quarrels as well as strong mutual attachments – no such favour is shown; the full legal remedy is claimed, and sometimes a situation develops where the people either resort to sorcery, or those who feel aggrieved move away.

There are hints in the literature that even among peoples said to have a stereotyped pattern of dealing with fratricides the norm is not always strictly observed. We have already seen, for example, that among the Bedouin of Sinai a father may use his influence to secure a reduction in the amount of bloodmoney payable to the next of kin; but, our source continues, if the father is dead, "the murderer would have to pay whatever his brother's next of kin demanded, or risk reprisals".[25] We are told, too, that among the Vugusu no compensation is payable if a man kills a member of his own sub-clan, and that after the usual purification ceremony the killer's relatives and neighbours resume social relations with him; tribal traditions, nevertheless, record instances in which a man's killing of his brother led to blood-feud and a split in the group.[26] Of the Nandi, similarly, we read that "although there is no indemnification for the killing of a clansfellow, there is likely to be a good deal of ill-feeling on the part of the injured family, which may persist till it results in a permanent severance of relations between the families concerned".[27]

The relative scarcity of recorded case-histories makes generalization hazardous. But I would venture the opinion that, in those societies where action lies with the relatives of the victim, seldom is any hard-and-fast rule invariably followed in regard to fratricide and other internal killings; the absence of mitigation of punishment reported for many such societies, and the more severe penalties reported for others, are unlikely to be the actual practice in every individual instance.

It can thus only in terms of the immediate domestic situation, I would suggest, that we can adequately explain the different sequels to the various cases of fratricide recorded in the OT. In the light of the story told by the woman of Tekoa, we must assume that vengeance was permissible in such cases. But what did in fact happen? When Abimelech killed all his brothers but the youngest, the survivor solemnly cursed him and then fled in fear, certainly in no position to take direct revenge. When Absalom killed Amnon – and he seems to have had ample provocation for his deed – David's other sons who were present at the time made no attempt to retaliate, but fled, presumably fearing that they too might be killed. Absalom himself then also fled, undoubtedly to escape punishment; but David, instead of pursuing, ultimately recalled and pardoned him – and most commentators have stressed the king's partiality for his favourite son as one of the grave defects in his character. When the woman of Tekoa's son killed his brother, her husband's relatives insisted on vengeance: but primarily, it is indicated, because they wished to secure the inheritance for themselves. She, on the other hand, did not share their sentiments, and successfully pleaded with the king to intervene. Solomon's killing of Adonijah and Jehoram's killing of all his brothers were, like Abimelech's deed, political assassinations, of a kind fairly common elsewhere (as among the southern Bantu, for example), and no doubt those two kings were well able to protect themselves had other members of the family thought of seeking revenge.

Cain's outlawry, it seems to me, is therefore not an example of a regular pattern such as Robertson Smith describes for the Arabs. It illustrates, rather, that what happened in cases of fratricide among the biblical Hebrews depended, not so much upon fixed legal rules, as upon the size and momentary composition of the family, the domestic balance of power, the circumstances of the killing, the personal feelings of the people involved, and other factors of the same general kind. Such factors must almost inevitably have weighed heavily in a social situation where the right of prosecution lay, not with a neutral political authority, but with people who were the nearest relatives not only of the person who had been killed but of the person by whom he had been killed.

If, again following orthodox belief, we assume that Cain was indeed a historical figure, then in a case such as his the domestic situation contained one other factor that might well have been decisive. The narrative describing Abimelech's death at the siege of Thebez ends with the words: "Thus God requited the crime of Abimelech, which he committed against his father in killing his seventy brothers" (Judg. 9:56); and the woman of Tekoa, when pleading for the life of her son, said that his death would leave to her husband "neither name nor remnant upon the face of the earth" (2 Sam. 14:7). Both passages illustrate the obvious importance attached by the biblical Hebrews to a man's having male descendants to perpetuate his memory; and in the well-known ordinance prescribing the levirate it is stated that if a man dies without a son, his brother should cohabit with the widow in order to raise seed to the deceased, "that his name may not be blotted out of Israel" (Deut. 25:5ff.). As Pedersen says, commenting on this passage, "If a man, after having contracted a marriage, dies without sons, then he dies entirely. It is this blotting out of life which is to be avoided."[28] It may reasonably be argued, therefore, that one reason for Cain's life having been spared was that, at the time, he was the only surviving son of his father, and his death would have meant the extinction of the family.

It is very tempting, finally, to assume that the uncertainty attaching to the treatment of fratricides was ultimately recognized as undesirable, and that they too were brought into the same category as all other homicides. In the Priestly Code the following passage occurs: "For your lifeblood I will surely require a reckoning; of every beast I will require it and of man; of every man's brother I will require the life of man" (Gen. 9:5). In view of what has already been said, one might well feel disposed to argue that here it is specifically decreed that fratricides are no longer to be allowed to escape the lawful penalty for their crime. But as virtually every commentator agrees that the words "of every man's brother" are to be interpreted as referring to the figurative brotherhood of all mankind, and not the sibling relationship, it is probably unwise to press the alternative explanation, fitting climax though it would have provided for the incidents that I have been discussing.

What I have tried to do here is to raise the problem of why fratricides in the OT, of whom Cain was perhaps the most notorious, should all have escaped lawful retaliation at the hands of a human avenger. I have not been concerned with the wider problem of why the biblical Hebrews treated homicide as a tort and not as a crime, and why they preferred blood-vengeance to compensation. Nor, on the other hand, have I aimed at providing an explanation that would apply to all the alleged instances of differentiation by primitive peoples between homicide generally and the killing of a kinsman in particular. That would require much more investigation, and above all many more authentic case-histories than seem to be available at present. But if I have succeeded in showing that some help towards the solution of our specific problem can be found by reference to comparative ethnography, then I shall have succeeded, too, I hope, in showing once again how useful is this approach to biblical studies – an approach whose value Frazer, in particular, was so ready to appreciate and so well able to prove in his writings.

NOTES

1 James G. Frazer, *Folk-Lore in the Old Testament*, vol. 1 (London: Macmillan, 1918) 78–103.

2 Samuel R. Driver, *The Book of Genesis*, 12th edn (London: 1926) 67.

3 Frazer, *Folk-Lore in the Old Testament*, 99.

4 Frazer, *Folk-Lore in the Old Testament*, 100f.

5 Cf. Gen. 22:1–19 (Abraham and Isaac); 42:37 (Reuben and his sons): Judg. 11:29–40 (Jephthah and his daughter); 1 Sam. 14:39, 44 (Saul and Jonathan).

6 The relevant biblical passages are summarized and discussed by, among others, Johs. Pedersen, *Israel: Its Life and Culture*, vol. 1–2 (London: H. Milford, 1926) 378ff.; David Daube, *Studies in Biblical Law* (Cambridge: CUP, 1947) 102ff.

7 Louis Ginzberg, *The Legends of the Jews*, vol. 1 (Philadelphia: Jewish Publication Society, 1947) 112.

8 Cf. Sebald R. Steinmetz, *Ethnologische Studien zur ersten Entwicklung der Strafe*, 2nd edn (Groningen: P. Noordhoff, 1928), esp. vol. 1, part 3; Edward Westermarck, *The Origin and Development of the Moral Ideas*, vol. 1 (London: Macmillan, 1906) ch. 20; William Seagle, *The Quest for Law* (New York: Alfred Knopf, 1941) chaps. 3 and 4.

9 Isaac Schapera, *The Khoisan Peoples of South Africa* (London: G. Routledge, 1930) 154f., 345f.

10 George W. B. Huntingford, *The Nandi of Kenya* (London: Routledge & Kegan Paul, 1953) 111ff.; John Middleton, *The Kikuyu and Kamba of Kenya* (London: International African Institute, 1953) 44f.; Guenter Wagner, "The Bantu of Kavirondo", in *African Political Systems*, ed. Meyer Fortes, Edward E. Evans-

Pritchard, 197–236 (London: OUP, 1940) 222ff.; Siegfried F. Nadel, *The Nuba* (London: OUP, 1947) 302f.

11 C. Wandres, "Über das Recht der Naman", *Zeitschrift für Kolonialpolitik* 11 (1909) 657–86, see p. 673.

12 William J. Burchell, *Travels in the Interior of Southern Africa*, vol. 1 (London: Batchworth Press, 1953) 319.

13 Nadel, *The Nuba*, 303.

14 W. Robertson Smith, *Lectures on the Religion of the Semites*, 3rd edn (London: A. & C. Black, 1927) 419ff.; *Kinship and Marriage in Early Arabia*, new edn (London: A. & C. Black, 1907) 25. My quotations are a blend from the two sources.

15 Austin Kennett, *Bedouin Justice: Laws and Customs among the Egyptian Bedouin* (Cambridge: CUP, 1925) chap. 6, esp. p. 53.

16 Edmund H. Ashton, *The Basuto* (London: International African Institute, 1952) 255ff.; C. Hoffmann, "Rechtsgebräuche der Basuto", *Zeitschrift für Eingeborenensprachen* 24 (1934) 58–76.

17 Cf. Steinmetz, *Ethnologische Studien*, vol. 2, 151–63.

18 See, e.g., E. Durkheim and P. Fauconnet in book reviews in *L'Année Sociologique* 1 (1896/7) 353–8 and 5 (1900/1) 403.

19 Cf. Num. 35:33; Job 16:18; Isa. 26:21; Ezra 24:7ff.

20 Cf. Wagner, "The Bantu of Kavirondo", 218; Edward E. Evans-Pritchard, *The Nuer* (Oxford: OUP, 1940) 156.

21 In Exod. 21:30, 32 provision is made for the payment of compensation by a man whose ox has gored someone to death.

22 Evans-Pritchard, *The Nuer*, 150ff.; "The Nuer of the Southern Sudan", in *African Political Systems*, 272–96, see p. 292.

23 I have discussed the case, and several others like it, in "The Tswana Conception of Incest", in *Social Structure: Studies Presented to A. R. Radcliffe-Brown*, ed. Meyer Fortes, 104–20 (Oxford: Clarendon Press, 1949).

24 I cannot vouch for the accuracy of the data, which are paraphrased from the statements of informants who were not eye-witnesses of the incidents described.

25 Kennett, *Bedouin Justice*, 54.

26 Wagner, "The Bantu of Kavirondo". 218; *The Bantu of North Kavirondo* (London: International African Institute, 1949) 69.

27 Huntingford, *The Nandi of Kenya*, 113.

28 Pedersen, *Israel: Its Life and Culture*, 78.

3

*The Hebrew Conception of Corporate Personality: A Re-examination**

JOHN W. ROGERSON

It is nearly sixty years since H. Wheeler Robinson first suggested that corporate personality was an indispensable key for understanding ancient Hebrew thought.[1] It is a tribute to his influence on biblical studies that the idea continues to be used by scholars in various countries, and by New Testament scholars as well as OT scholars. However, in a recent article, J. R. Porter has sounded a note of warning:

> The expression (corporate personality) has become something of a commonplace. But commonplaces are always dangerous, not least in the realm of scholarship; and that for two reasons. First, the exact force and significance of a commonplace expression tends to be rapidly forgotten, and it soon takes the place of original research and original thought. Secondly, the very convenience and ease of such an expression means that it tends to become applied to aspects of the subject under discussion for which it was never really suited.[2]

Porter's article is confined to an examination of passages from the OT on the basis of which Robinson maintained that corporate personality was operative in Hebrew legal practice. In every case, Porter suggests an alternative explanation, and concludes that while corporate personality may play a vital part in non-legal contexts in the OT, it is very much to be doubted whether Hebrew law is concerned with the "psychic community" or "psychical unity" that the theory of corporate personality demands.

---

*First published in *JTS* 21 (1970) 1–16. In the interest of brevity the notes have been slightly abridged.

The obvious way of examining the subject further is to take Porter's article for granted, and to examine the non-legal uses of corporate personality in the same way that he examines the legal uses. However, this would assume that we know exactly what is meant by corporate personality – but can we assume this? An examination of Robinson's many writings reveals the surprising fact that although he was using a term taken from English law[3] to describe a phenomenon "to which our thought and language have no real parallel"[4] he nowhere defined exactly what he meant. Rather, he defined the concept from time to time, usually when he made use of it to solve a particular problem, but as far as I know, he devoted no one single work to an exposition of corporate personality in all its ramifications. Accordingly, the aim of this article is not to begin where Porter left off but to try to establish the meaning of corporate personality. Moreover, I shall try to show that there was from the outset an ambiguity in Robinson's use of the phrase, and that this ambiguity enabled him to apply the concept to periods of Israel's history when one would have expected this survival from Israel's primitive past to have vanished. Further, I shall try to show that this ambiguity has enabled other scholars to make use of the theory in a way for which it was never really suited.

The method of the article will be to examine Robinson's important early writings on the subject (his later writings were merely elaborations of a theory regarded as already well established) and to discuss the extent to which the theory must stand or fall with the anthropological views on which it was based. At the outset, however, it is necessary to anticipate an objection to this approach. It may be argued that what is relevant is the applicability of corporate personality to the OT,[5] and that to examine the anthropological theories on which corporate personality was based is to commit the genetic fallacy. However, the matter is not quite so simple. Porter's article shows that the same OT passages can be explained in different ways. Where the subject-matter involves ancient or primitive thought-forms, how can we judge which explanation is correct? (Both might, of course, be incorrect.) Surely we can turn to anthropology and say at least that any explanation that would not be accepted by anthropologists in other contexts is unlikely to be correct in the context of the OT. Or to put it another way, it is doubtful whether Robinson would have thought of interpreting parts of the OT in terms of corporate personality if he had not been indebted to anthropological theories current in his younger years. If these theories have now been modified or abandoned by subsequent research, surely it is perilous not to ask how corporate personality is thereby affected.

Robinson's first use of the phrase was in *The Christian Doctrine of Man*, but the idea was already clearly present in his mind when he wrote his commentary on Deuteronomy and Joshua in the Century Bible, published four years earlier. In the introduction to Joshua, Robinson argued that the Achan incident (Josh. 7) illustrated the "non-individualistic or corporate idea of personality" which he amplified with the words "the whole family exterminated, just as the whole of Israel suffered".[6]

It is not difficult to guess where Robinson got this idea from. In his introduction to Deuteronomy, he refers extensively to Sir Henry Maine's *Ancient Law* and applies Maine's theory of the three-stage development of Indo-European law to Semitic, and especially, OT law.[7] Now in the chapter entitled "Primitive Society and Ancient Law", Maine describes primitive society as an aggregation of groups; he discusses the Roman institution of *patria potestas*, and traces the gradual emergence of the Law of Persons. In the following chapter on Testamentary Succession he likens the family in primitive society to a corporation aggregate; he reiterates that primitive society has for its units not individuals but groups, and points out that the narrowest personal relation in which a man stood was that of the family. "A man was never regarded as *himself*, as a distinct individual. His individuality was swallowed up in his family."[8] When we bear in mind the fact that corporate personality in English law is concerned with corporations aggregate, it is easy to see the influence of Maine on Robinson's phrase "non-individualistic or corporate idea of personality" which was later to become "corporate personality".

Two points must be noted here. First, there is no suggestion in Maine that in primitive society a man had no consciousness that he was an individual. The point is that a man had no individual rights. He was protected by his social group and not by an independent judiciary maintaining his individual rights. This is an important point, because the theory of corporate personality as applied to the OT was to make assertions about the way a man was conscious of himself as an individual within his social group. Maine was not concerned with how a man regarded *himself*, but with how he was regarded by society. His concern was law, not psychology.

Second, there is an incongruity in Robinson's use of Doughty's *Arabia Deserta* immediately after his use of Maine. Robinson quoted Doughty in order to illustrate from nineteenth-century Bedouin practice "the picture of primitive Semitic legislation preserved by the changeless desert".[9] However, he overlooked one important fact, namely, that while the societies described by Maine had developed from the patriarchal family with the power of the father over his children, this institution hardly existed, if at all, in Bedouin society. Instead, the probable practice of parallel cousin marriage severely weakened the family unit.[10] According to W. Robertson Smith it was a great mistake to suppose that Arab society is based on the patriarchal authority of the father over his sons; on the contrary "there is no part of the world where parental authority is weaker than in the desert".[11] Robinson is not to be blamed for this incongruity; it was commonly believed at the time that all societies had evolved in the same way, and thus anthropologists synthesized factors from societies widely different from each other in social structure. At the same time, it must be noted that this sort of procedure greatly assisted the development of the notion of corporate personality.

In *The Christian Doctrine of Man*, Robinson used the phrase corporate personality to express in a positive way what J. B. Mozley, himself clearly dependent on Maine, had called "the defective sense of individuality" said to be common among the ancients.[12] By way of further clarification, Robinson explained that "we find men dealt with, in primitive legislation and religion, not on the basis of the single life which consciousness binds together for each one of us, but as members of a tribe, a clan, or a family; hence ... the idea that the sin of one (e.g. Achan) can properly be visited on the group to which he belongs, and into which his own personality, so to speak, extends".[13] Now had Robinson merely stated that in primitive legislation men were dealt with not on the basis of the single life, but as members of a tribe, a clan, or a family, it would have been clear what he meant by corporate personality. He would have been saying that an individual had no rights, but was protected by his social group, and was held responsible, though innocent to our way of thinking, for an action of the head of the group, or one of its members. The phrase "corporate responsibility", used to explain the Achan incident in the commentary on Joshua,[14] would have expressed this perfectly.

However, it is important to note the two phrases "the single life which consciousness binds together for each one of us" and "into which his own personality, so to speak, extends". The meaning of the first phrase is not exactly clear to me, but it seems to suggest that we today have an awareness of being an individual that the primitive did not have. The second phrase suggests that the primitive was not aware as we are today of the limits of his own personality, and that he could think of this as extending into the group to which he belonged. It is obvious that these statements, if interpreted correctly, go beyond corporate responsibility. They represent an attempt to give a psychological explanation for corporate responsibility, and in so doing they make assertions about the psychology of primitives, and suggest that primitives were unable to distinguish between the individual and his group in the way that we do. For this psychological explanation, Robinson was dependent not on Maine, but on anthropological theory.

In *The Christian Doctrine of Man* Robinson referred to Spencer and Gillen's *The Northern Tribes of Central Australia* which describes societies dominated by the ideas of identity of substance between the clan and the eponymous totem, and the magico-biological unity of members of the same clan.[15] On the assumption that one could apply these features of the life of Australian aborigines to the Hebrews, Robinson's psychological explanation of corporate personality was reasonable, and to be fair to him, not only was this sort of use of anthropological material familiar in his day, but his researches into Hebrew psychological terms had convinced him that Hebrew psychology was essentially that of primitive societies.[16] However, it is here that the ambiguity referred to at the beginning of the article can be discerned. The psychological explanation of corporate responsibility is not only an explanation; it is itself part of the meaning of corporate personality, which thus denotes two things: (i) corporate responsibility and (ii) a psychical unity between members of the same social group, in which the limits of an individual's personality are not clearly defined. This ambiguity depends on the combination of ideas from Maine and anthropology.

A tension can be discerned between these two senses of corporate personality in *The Christian Doctrine of Man*. On the one hand, the OT is said to show a progression from corporate personality "to the recognition of moral responsibility".[17] The phrase clearly denotes corporate responsibility here. On the other hand, in a discussion of St Paul's teaching, it is claimed that "Adam is the 'corporate personality' of the race, over against Christ as the corporate personality of his body, the Church".[18] Clearly, the idea of corporate responsibility is inappropriate here, and what is being asserted is that there is a psychical unity between Adam and the

47

human race, and between Christ and the members of the Church.

It is important to ask how Robinson was able to maintain at one and the same time that corporate personality was a primitive survival in Hebrew thought that was gradually superseded by individual moral responsibility, and that in the first century A.D., the idea was still operative in Hebrew thought. The answer is to be found in his discussion of the rise of individualism from the eighth-century prophets onwards. The doctrine of Ezekiel that "the soul that sinneth, it shall die" could, according to Robinson, have led to results as immoral as those springing from corporate personality, if it has been understood that every suffering experienced by a person was the result of punishment for sin. One had to allow for the suffering of the innocent person because of his involvement in society. Thus Robinson argued that the theory of individual responsibility came to be combined with that of corporate person-ality, so that "the individualism of the Old Testament is usually, if not always, conceived as realised in and through the society which is based upon it".[19] However, what sense of corporate personality is required if we are to talk meaningfully of combining the concept with that of individual responsibility? On the face of it, corporate responsibility seems to fit, but in fact it only fits in a different sense from that given the phrase by Robinson. By corporate responsibility he meant that a member of a group could be held fully responsible for an action of the group, though he personally had done nothing, *because he was not regarded as an individual.* The sense required is that an individual can suffer innocently by being caught up with the fortunes of the society to which he belongs. A difficulty also exists with the second sense of corporate personality, which depends on the inability of the individual clearly to recognize the limits of his own personality. Individual responsibility can hardly be com-bined with the inability of the Hebrews to discern the exact limits of an individual life. One is left with the conclusion that Robinson's attempt to prolong the life of corporate personality beyond the exile depends on another shift in meaning of the phrase, this meaning being that a man cannot be treated as an isolated individual, but must be viewed as a member of society. This sense depends on neither Maine nor anthropology, but on a modern understanding of man and his community. Indeed, the plausibility of this part of the argument depends on its being self-evident to modern readers.

In Robinson's later writings, it was the second sense that assumed the greatest prominence. One of the main reasons for this was that Robinson was influenced by the writings of L. Lévy-Bruhl.[20] Lévy-

Bruhl was responsible for the theory that primitives thought in a pre-logical way. They could not, it was alleged, distinguish between different objects, or between objective and subjective experiences such as dreams and reality. They experienced the world in a mystical sort of way which ran contrary to our Western ideas of logical thought. In spite of the fact that it may be questioned whether Lévy-Bruhl himself would have regarded the Hebrews as primitives,[21] Robinson made use of his writings to elaborate the idea that the primitive Israelite had no clear idea of the limits of his own personality within the social group. At the same time, Robinson transferred his attention from social institutions and customs strange to modern readers, and thereby calling out for explanation, to parts of the OT where it was possible to "find" corporate personality, although the subjects concerned could be quite satisfactorily explained in other ways. He also began to use the theory to reconcile the conflicting views of modern scholarship.

In a paper read to the Society for Old Testament Study in 1923, Robinson suggested that in prophetic experience, a prophet's personality was so merged with that of God, that he could "stand in the place of God, and speak for him with absolute conviction".[22] He expressed the view that "corporate representation" (note the phrase!) figured as largely in Hebrew prophecy as in Hebrew law. In later writings he developed this line of thought even further. He used corporate personality to support the view that the prophet was conceived as being present in Yahweh's heavenly court,[23] and in one remarkable passage suggested that the prophet looked at the world through God's eyes. "Their (the prophets') organs became the very organs of God. They felt the beating of God's heart as their own; their eyes became the eyes of God seeing things unseen by men; their ears rang with the cry of human rebellion as though they were his. *All this was no figure of speech to them.*"[24] Such a claim could rest only on the assumption that Hebrew thought processes resembled those of Lévy-Bruhl's primitives.

In the same paper, Robinson listed without comment the songs of the Servant of Yahweh together with his usual "proofs" (from the realm of Hebrew law) for corporate personality in the OT.[25] In *The Cross of the Servant* this was worked out more fully. Two points are noteworthy. First, Robinson again directly acknowledged his debt to anthropology in the work of Spencer and Gillen, and Lévy-Bruhl, and second, he used corporate personality to resolve differences of scholarly opinion. The isolation of four Servant songs, though widely accepted, is the result of modern scholarship. The need to impose a unified interpretation on them stems from the same quarter. But how can one reconcile the individualistic fourth song with the statement in the second that the Servant is Israel (Isa. 49:3)? Robinson used corporate personality to say, in effect, that scholars who held to an individualistic interpretation, and those who held to a collective interpretation, were both right. How corporate personality could maintain this is clear from the following quotation:

> There is a fluidity of conception, a possibility of swift transition from the one to the many, and vice versa, to which our thought and language have no real parallel. When we do honour today to the 'Unknown Warrior' we can clearly distinguish between the particular soldier buried in the Abbey and the great multitude of whom we have consciously made him the representative. But that clearness of distinction would have been lacking to an earlier world, prior to the development of the modern sense of personality.[26]

The thought here is that just as the Hebrew mind would not be able to distinguish between the unknown warrior and those he represents, so the writer of the Servant poems could not distinguish between the Servant and the community to which he belonged, and hence, there is a fluidity of thought from the one to the other. Individual and collective interpretations of the Servant of Yahweh have thus been emphasizing different aspects of this fluidity of thought.

So far, I have tried to ascertain the meaning of corporate personality as used by Robinson, and have tried to point out the ambiguity involved in this usage. It must be admitted, however, that this ambiguity is not in itself fatal to Robinson's arguments. If indeed there was a development in Israel's life from corporate responsibility to moral individuality, and if Hebrew thought really was similar to that of Lévy-Bruhl's primitives, these facts cannot be invalidated just because Robinson combined them under the umbrella of corporate personality. The need is for the two questions to be examined on their own merits. However, since Porter has already examined the cases in the OT claimed by Robinson to support corporate responsibility, there is no need to duplicate his work. I shall be concerned, therefore, with the second question, but as explained earlier, I shall not discuss the OT material, but the anthropological theory on which the interpretation of OT material was based.

As has been seen, Robinson's greatest dependence was on the

theories of Lévy-Bruhl about primitive mentality. It is safe to say that in anthropological circles today, while Lévy-Bruhl is regarded as having posed some important questions which must still be faced, his actual theories about primitive mentality are seriously questioned. Apart from the observation that if his theories were true "we would scarcely be able to communicate with primitives, even to learn their languages"[27] (an observation which also would presumably hold good for the ancient Hebrews, if they thought like primitives), there are several main criticisms of his theories. First, he was not a field anthropologist, and therefore had little first-hand experience of the people he was describing. Second, he used a scissors-and-paste method of writing which indiscriminately forced material from widely differing cultures and periods into elementary classifications. Third, he ignored negative evidence, such as the fact that many primitive peoples do not at all bother about their shadows or their names. Fourth, he generalized about primitive people instead of examining variations in social structure and relating them to concomitant variations in the patterns of thought.[28] Fifth, the phenomena he sought to explain have been more satisfactorily explained in other ways by field anthropologists.

To illustrate this last point, it is worth noting how E. E. Evans-Pritchard, who did much to try to understand Lévy-Bruhl, and whose own studies of primitive peoples have become classics, has dealt with the problem of what the Nuer mean when they say that a twin is a bird. Having questioned the Nuer about this statement, and having investigated the circumstances in which it is made, he has reached the following conclusion.

> Anthropological explanations display two main errors. The first, best exemplified in the writings of Lévy-Bruhl, is that when a people say that something is something else which is different they are contravening the law of contradictories and substituting for it a law of their own prelogical way of thinking, that of mystical participations. I hope at least to have shown that Nuer do not assert identity between the two things. They may say that one is the other and in certain other situations act towards it as though it were that other, or something like it, but they are aware, no doubt with varying degrees of awareness, and readily say, though with varying degrees of clarity and emphasis, that the two things are different.[29]

Two points must be noted from these criticisms of Lévy-Bruhl. First, contemporary anthropologists are doubtful whether Lévy-Bruhl's explanation of the phenomena on which he based his theory of primitive mentality was correct. Second, his indiscriminate use of material from widely differing cultures is no longer acceptable. With regard to corporate personality, the question mark put against Lévy-Bruhl's theories must also be put against Robinson's use of corporate personality in its second sense. Further, if primitives were known whose thought processes did resemble those assumed by the theory of prelogical mentality, this would not justify corporate personality unless the culture and social organization of the people concerned closely resembled that of the Hebrews. It is obvious that the natives of Central Australia would hardly fit the bill, and it is to be doubted whether nineteenth-century Bedouin do either. The onus of proof rests on present-day exponents of corporate personality to show that their interpretation of OT material would not be rejected by anthropologists if applied to material with which the latter are familiar.

If corporate personality in its second sense is thus seriously questioned, this affects not only Robinson, but others who have used corporate personality, since it is the second sense of the theory that has been almost exclusively employed. The work of two scholars in particular deserves attention, namely D. S. Russell and A. R. Johnson. In his book *The Method and Message of Jewish Apocalyptic* Russell has explained the phenomenon of pseudonymity in terms of corporate personality. He writes:

> we have seen reason to suppose that the apocalyptic writer shared a sense of kinship with the ancient seer in whose name he wrote ... May it not be that, by thus appropriating his name the writer thought of himself as in some way an "extension" of his personality along the lines indicated above? If such were the case his sense of "identification" would be much more complete than would otherwise be the case, for by assuming his name he would thereby be sharing in his very life and character.[30]

It should be noted that there is nothing in the phenomenon of pseudonymity that calls for its explanation in these terms. The use of corporate personality is quite unnecessary, and is completely dependent on Lévy-Bruhl's theory of primitive mentality.

Johnson has made use of corporate personality in order to maintain theories about the relation of Yahweh to his messengers, the relation of the king to Yahweh and the king to the Israelite people, and has even suggested that it may help to give us a new approach to the extension of Jewish Monotheism in the direction of later Trinitarianism.[31] Johnson's position needs careful scrutiny because he denies that he is dependent on the theories of Lévy-Bruhl.[32] He writes, "the adoption of an element in Lévy-Bruhl's terminology should not be held to imply an acceptance of his associated theories, especially that of a 'prelogical' mentality or even that of a 'law of participation'".[33] Johnson even notes some early criticisms of Lévy-Bruhl, as well as the latter's partial renunciation of his theories. Again, in explanation of his statement that the mental activity of the Israelites was "predominantly synthetic" he writes, "while thus retaining my expression 'predominantly synthetic', I should like to stress the adverb 'predominantly' which was intended from the first as a safeguard against appearing to overlook the analytical aspects of Israelite thinking".[34]

The difficulty with all this is that one is not clear what Johnson is trying to maintain. What does it mean to say that the mental processes of the Israelites were "predominantly synthetic"? In what respects were they analytic? How can we be sure that a description of a psychological term such as *nephesh* in terms of synthetic thought is correct? Would a description in terms of analytic thinking be incorrect, and if so why? This is not the only difficulty. The latest edition of *Sacral Kingship in Ancient Israel* is more recent than that of *The Vitality of the Individual* in which Johnson's explanations quoted above appear. However, in *Sacral Kingship* we read, "It is necessary to bear in mind that in Israelite thought, as in that of the so-called 'primitive' peoples of our own day, there is a vivid sense of what has been called 'corporate personality'."[35] If Johnson rejects Lévy-Bruhl's theories of primitive mentality, on what does he base this assertion about primitive peoples of our own day? In fact he bases it, according to the footnotes, on Robinson, whose indebtedness to Lévy-Bruhl is openly acknowledged. It is thus difficult to escape the conclusion that in claiming not to accept Lévy-Bruhl's theories of primitive mentality, Johnson is simply tidying up his footnotes so as to avoid the charge of not being aware of the serious questioning of Lévy-Bruhl's theories. What is actually called for is a radical examination of how the questioning of Lévy-Bruhl affects theories about Israelite mental processes. In any case, Johnson's application of the mental processes of primitives to Israelite thought is, as we have seen, unacceptable.

Before leaving Johnson, another statement of his must be noted. In *The One and the Many* he comments on the oscillation between singular and plural in Num. 20:14–21. "Of course, we sometimes betray a similar oscillation when we have occasion, for example, to think of a committee; but our thinking is not so dominated by this point of view as that of the Israelites seems to have been."[36] This comment is interesting because it admits that far from being the result of sharing the mental processes of primitives, this oscillation in Hebrew thought is something known to modern Western society. Yet Robinson had described it as something "to which our thought and language have no real parallel". Nor is Johnson's the only example of such a statement. H. H. Rowley, while accepting Robinson's interpretation of the "I" of the Psalms in terms of corporate personality has written, "The Psalms expressed the worship of all, but they also expressed the worship of each, *just as individuals and congregations today* make these ancient Psalms the vehicle of their individual and corporate approach to God."[37] It is odd that it should be possible to make such a close comparison between ancient and modern corporate use of the Psalms if the Hebrew mind analysed the relation of the individual to his group in such a different way from ourselves.

Again, R. P. Shedd, who assumed a "marked contrast between ancient Semitic thought and the modern Western mind"[38] uses a quotation from C. H. Dodd to explain the Hebrew view of personality. The quotation is "In actual fact, human personality, as we know it in ourselves, is not simple, but indefinitely complex. In particular it is constituted out of personal relations. From the beginning of our individual existence we throw out tentacles, as it were, to other persons, and they throw out tentacles to us." Shedd continues, "It is primarily in this area of thought that the Hebrew conception of the unity of the community lies."[39] Once more we note the odd way in which modern experience is appealed to in order to support a phenomenon supposed to be quite outside the range of modern experience.

What is the reason for these odd arguments? It is clearly lack of attention to the importance of social context in trying to establish the nature of both Hebrew and Western thought. The Hebrew thought which is allegedly so different from our own is not just based on the application to Israel of alleged mental processes of primitives; it is also an abstraction from those Israelite institutions which corporate responsibility sought to explain, formed into an entity labelled "Hebrew thought" and then imposed on the rest of the OT regardless of social context. At the same time, it is assumed without discussion, and again without reference to social context, that modern Western thought is individualistic.

That this will not do will be obvious from a moment's reflection on modern experiences. A Standard Average European[40] *can* be deeply concerned for the well-being of his president or his monarch; he *can* identify himself with the needs and hopes of his family, his town or his country as the context determines. In the 1966 World Cup Association Football final between England and West Germany, a considerable number of Englishmen found themselves desperately involved in the fortunes of their team which stood for England in a very real sense. Thus it will be seen that corporate personality in its second sense has not only depended on the theories of Lévy-Bruhl, but also on unexamined generalizations about Hebrew thought and Western thought.

If I have succeeded in showing that corporate personality is an ambiguous term, that this ambiguity has been responsible for the application of the theory to the later as well as the earlier parts of the OT, and that the predominant use of the theory has been based on anthropological views that can no longer be maintained, the question is raised whether the term should be retained in OT studies. There is, of course, one way in which it might be defined and retained. Anthropologists are familiar with the term "corporate" as applied to certain lineage or descent groups. These groups consist of the descendants of a common ancestor; they are corporate in the sense that they are groups that exist independently of the individuals composing them; sometimes they act as a body in blood feud, and sometimes they hold land which cannot be alienated by an individual member. It might, therefore, be possible to redefine corporate personality along these lines, and apply it to blood feud, levirate marriage, and the idea of descent from a common ancestor. Indeed, Robinson used corporate personality to explain the idea of common descent, although probably this explanation was strongly influenced by the theory of primitive mentality.[41] However, such a redefinition would be unwise in my view, for three reasons. First, anthropologists are not clear what they mean by corporateness. A recent writer comments, "The concept of corporateness, as used in the ethnographic literature, is confused and ambiguous, and urgently needs clarification."[42] Second, not all lineage or descent groups have the features outlined above. Third, we probably know insufficient of the tribal and lineage system of the ancient Hebrews to make valid inferences from other societies to Israelite society. In the interests of clarity it would therefore be best to drop the term corporate personality completely, and at the same time to abandon any attempt to explain OT phenomena in terms of primitive mentality.

It must be noted that while such a move would fundamentally question theories such as pseudonymity in apocalyptic, prophetic experience in which the prophet cannot distinguish between himself and God and himself and Israel, messengers human or divine being extensions of the personality of their master, and probably the work of Robinson and Johnson on Hebrew psychology, some OT material explained by corporate personality would not be affected in the same way. In particular, the "I" of the Psalms and the idea of the hopes of the people being centred in the king would be affected differently. This is because in these cases, corporate personality was not used to point out a tension between collective and individual, but to explain what could be seen in the OT in any case. Robinson was not the first to suggest that the "I" of the Psalms was the corporate body of the nation or the community. He simply tried to explain the suggestion with reference to corporate personality. In so doing he added nothing but confusion, because on the one hand he convinced himself and his followers that primitive mentality could be clearly found in the OT, and on the other hand he obscured the fact pointed out by Rowley that the corporate use of "I" was something known to modern worshippers. Similarly, the dropping of corporate personality does not affect the fact that the hopes of the Israelites were centred on their king. What it does imply is that these hopes depended on something other than the inability to distinguish clearly between the king and the community of which he was head.

The question of the Servant songs is slightly more complex. My own view of the songs is that the first three were written by Deutero-Isaiah, and that the Servant in them is the prophetic circle of which the author was head. The fourth song is by a different author, one of the prophetic circle, and describes the career of Deutero-Isaiah himself. Given this view, I am prepared to see a tension between collective and individual in the following sense. The prophetic circle is the ideal Israel, and in this way represents Israel. At the same time, the prophet Deutero-Isaiah bears the brunt of the activity of the prophetic circle so that he is regarded by the latter as the Servant himself. Thus there is a tension between an individual prophet, his immediate circle, and the whole nation for which they stand. This view, however, is based on a study of the texts of Deutero-Isaiah, and does not involve any appeal to primitive mentality. The extent to which it differs from theories based on corporate personality can be seen by reference to C. R. North's *The Suffering Servant in Deutero-Isaiah*. North seems to take the "ebb and flow" of Hebrew thought as suggested by Robinson so much for granted, that he is concerned to argue about the *direction* of this ebb and flow. He writes: "As I understand him [Robinson], the 'ebb and flow' of Deutero-Isaiah's thought was from Israel to his own prophetic consciousness, *and back to Israel.* As I see it, the direction was rather from collective Israel to an individual who was neither himself nor anyone else who had lived hitherto ... The figure is a pyramid, not a circle."[43] Here the use of ideas of primitive mentality has led to an absurd discussion, with conclusions that cannot be verified in any conceivable way.

By allowing that in spite of the dropping of corporate personality there are certain parts of the Old Testament where there is a tension between the collective and the individual that has to be explained, I am not saying that Robinson and his followers reached the correct conclusions by the wrong methods. On the contrary, I hope to have shown that many of the conclusions reached were wrong. The way in which such tensions can be explained may, however, have been indicated unwittingly by Rowley, Johnson, and Shedd in their references to modern experience as illuminating the collective and the individual. However, this is not to be understood as though I were saying that for corporate personality one must substitute reference to modern experience. The latter may help us understand some passages that are otherwise explained by corporate personality, but as shown above in the discussion of the Servant songs, the explanation will differ considerably from that in terms of primitive mentality. Also, I must not be held to mean that anthropology must no longer be used to illuminate the OT. We still have much to learn from anthropology about such subjects as sacrifice and ritual, and the nature and meaning of mythology. In short, although his work has been dated by the advance of knowledge in the field of anthropology, H. Wheeler Robinson by his application of anthropology to OT studies marked out a path which some scholars must today follow anew.

NOTES

1 Henry Wheeler Robinson, *The Christian Doctrine of Man* (Edinburgh: T. & T. Clark, 1911) 8.

2 J. R. Porter, "The Legal Aspects of the Concept of 'Corporate Personality' in the Old Testament", *VT* 15 (1965) 361–80; see p. 361.

3 H. W. Robinson, "The Hebrew Conception of Corporate Personality", in *Werden und Wesen des Alten Testaments* (BZAW 66; Berlin: Töpelmann, 1936) 49–62, see p. 51; reprinted in H. W. Robinson, *Corporate Personality in Ancient*

Israel, rev. edn (Philadelphia: Fortress, 1980), 25–44. For a legal exposition of the term see W. M. Geldart, *Elements of English Law*, 6th edn (London: OUP, 1959) 78ff.

4 H. W. Robinson, *The Cross in the Old Testament* (London: SCM, 1955) 77.

5 H. H. Rowley, *The Servant of the Lord and Other Essays*, 2nd edn (Oxford: Blackwell, 1965) 40.

6 H. W. Robinson, *Deuteronomy and Joshua* (Edinburgh: T. C. & E. C. Jack, 1907) 266.

7 Robinson, *Deuteronomy and Joshua*, 18.

8 Henry Maine, *Ancient Law*, 12th edn (London: J. Murray, 1888) 183.

9 Robinson, *Deuteronomy and Joshua*, 19.

10 R. F. Murphy and L. Kasdon, "The Structure of Parallel Cousin Marriage", *AA* 41 (1959) 17–29.

11 W. Robertson Smith, *Kinship and Marriage in Early Arabia* (Cambridge: CUP, 1885) 56.

12 James B. Mozley, *Ruling Ideas in Early Ages*, new edn (London: Longmans, 1900) 87.

13 Robinson, *The Christian Doctrine of Man*, 8.

14 Robinson, *Deuteronomy and Joshua*, 300. Mozley is quoted also at this point.

15 Baldwin Spencer and F. J. Gillen, *The Northern Tribes of Central Australia* (London: Macmillan, 1904).

16 Robinson, *The Christian Doctrine of Man*, 11ff. It needs to be asked whether Robinson's explanation of Hebrew psychological terms was influenced by anthropology, and also to what extent the view that the centre of consciousness in a person could move rapidly from one physiological organ to another, is bound up with that explanation of corporate personality in which any member of a social group can become the embodiment of that group.

17 Robinson, *The Christian Doctrine of Man*, 11.

18 Robinson, *The Christian Doctrine of Man*, 121.

19 Robinson, *The Christian Doctrine of Man*, 34.

20 See, e.g., Lucien Lévy-Bruhl, *Primitive Mentality* (London: G. Allen & Unwin, 1923), and *How Natives Think* (London: G. Allen & Unwin, 1926). For Robinson's acknowledgement of his indebtedness to Lévy-Bruhl see *The Cross in the Old Testament*, 76.

21 Lévy-Bruhl, *Primitive Mentality*, 433.

22 H. W. Robinson, "The Psychology and Metaphysics of 'Thus Saith Yahweh'", *ZAW* 41 (1923) 1–15.

23 H. W. Robinson, *Inspiration and Revelation in the Old Testament* (Oxford: Clarendon Press, 1946) 169f.

24 H. W. Robinson, *The Old Testament, its Making and Meaning* (London: Univ. of London Press, 1937), 78. Emphasis added.

25 Robinson, "The Psychology and Metaphysics ...", 10.

26 Robinson, *The Cross in the Old Testament*, 77.

27 Edward E. Evans-Pritchard, *Theories of Primitive Religion* (Oxford: Clarendon Press, 1965) 87; cf. 9f. and 88.

28 Mary Douglas, *Purity and Danger* (London: Routledge & Kegan Paul, 1966) 75.

29 E. E. Evans-Pritchard, "A Problem of Nuer Religious Thought", *Sociologus* 4 (1954) 23–41 = *Myth and Cosmos*, ed. John Middleton (Garden City: N.Y.: Natural History Press, 1967) 145.

30 D. S. Russell, *The Method and Message of Jewish Apocalyptic* (London: SCM, 1964) 138.

31 A. R. Johnson, *The One and the Many in the Israelite Conception of God*, 2nd edn (Cardiff: Univ. of Wales Press, 1961) 28ff., 37; *Sacral Kingship in Ancient Israel*, 2nd edn (Cardiff: Univ. of Wales Press, 1967) 3f., 16ff.

32 Johnson often seems to use "extension of personality" in a distinct way from corporate personality, as though he has separated the two senses in which Robinson used the latter phrase. However, this is not consistently done, and since he is dependent on Lévy-Bruhl for the idea of "extension of personality" my argument is not affected. See A. R. Johnson, *The Vitality of the Individual in the Thought of Ancient Israel*, 2nd edn (Cardiff: Univ. of Wales Press, 1964) 3 note 3.

33 Johnson, *The Vitality of the Individual*, 1 note 4.

34 Johnson, *The Vitality of the Individual*, 2 note 1.

35 Johnson, *Sacral Kingship*, 2.

36 Johnson, *The One and the Many*, 12.

37 H. H. Rowley, *Worship in Ancient Israel* (London: SPCK, 1967) 249. Emphasis added.

38 Russell P. Shedd, *Man in Community: A Study of St. Paul's Application of Old Testament and Early Jewish Conceptions of Human Solidarity* (London: Epworth, 1958) 4.

39 Shedd, *Man in Community*, 4f.

40 A concept used by Benjamin Whorf as a basis of comparison with certain primitive cultures. See *Language and Culture*, ed. Harry Hoijer (Chicago: Univ. of Chicago Press, 1954) 47.

41 Robinson, "The Hebrew Concept of Corporate Personality", 51.

42 George P. Murdock, "Cognatic Forms of Social Organization", in *Social Structure in Southeast Asia*, ed. G. P. Murdock, 1–14 (Chicago: Quadrangle Books, 1960) 4.

43 C. R. North, *The Suffering Servant in Deutero-Isaiah*, 2nd edn (London: OUP, 1965) 215f.

4

*Prophecy: The Problem of Cross-Cultural Comparison**

THOMAS W. OVERHOLT

The phenomenon of prophecy has been widely distributed through-out human societies. We have recorded instances of prophetic activity from an impressive range of times and places, from the ancient Mesopotamian city-state of Mari, where in the eighteenth century B.C.E. prophets confronted royal administrators with the demands and promises of the god, to the New Yorker Joseph Smith, whose revelation and message have formed the basis for the development of Mormonism. The Saint-Simon movement of early nineteenth-century France is another of the many instances of prophecy that have arisen within the Western stream of tradition, but prophetic activity has also been extremely widespread outside that tradition. Since the late nineteenth century the peoples of Melanesia have produced a whole series of Cargo cult movements in most of which prophetic figures were of central importance. There were Tokerua, the "prophet of Milne Bay" (Papua, 1893); Saibai, the prophet of the German Wislin movement (Torres Straits, 1913); Evara and Biere of the Vailala Madness (Papua, 1919); and Manehevi and his successors in the John Frum movement (Tanna, 1939–present); to name but a few. Prophets have appeared in Africa, wartime Japan, among various American Indian groups and in other parts of the world as well.

Nor has the appearance of prophets been confined to a particular kind of cultural adjustment. To be sure, the term "prophet" is likely first to call to mind the great high civilizations of the ancient Near East and figures like Isaiah, Jeremiah, and Mohammed. But Wovoka, the prophet of the Ghost Dance religion of 1890, was a

---

*First published in *Semeia* 21 (1982) 55–78. In the interest of brevity the notes have been slightly abridged.

Nevada Paiute, a tribe whose simple hunting and gathering culture had only recently come into close contact with European civilization. Navosavakadua, the first prophet of the new Tuka religion among Fijians, began his movement about 1885 in an interior region where there were as yet no white settlements.

As one begins to explore the vast literature on prophecy, certain tendencies appear. For one thing, data from primitive and higher cultures are usually dealt with separately. Studies of the OT prophets, for example, normally make reference to extra-Israelite phenomena only to the extent that they bear directly on the development of Israelite prophecy. Much of the continuing discussion of the Mari prophets has centred on the question of the extent to which they were parallel in nature and function to the Israelite prophets, and one finds a similar concern mirrored in discussions of cult prophecy, and other possible institutional analogues to OT prophecy such as the royal messenger and royal vizier. On the other hand, one finds studies of prophecy that are confined to its appearance within "lower cultures" or among "colonial peoples".

Another tendency of the literature is to discuss prophecy less for its own sake than as an element in some larger process. Studies of the OT prophets have been very much preoccupied with the content of what these men proclaimed, and have found their message useful in helping to define the nature of Yahweh and his relationship to his people, as well as the general development of Israelite culture and religion. Thus we have discussions of "prophecy and covenant", and of the relationship of prophecy to certain specific aspects of Israelite culture. This inclination to be more interested in the theological content of the proclamation than in the prophetic process itself is particularly evident in some of the well-known "theologies" of the OT.

When one turns to extra-Israelite phenomena, the situation is similar. The focus is not so much on prophecy itself as on the broader socio-cultural movements of which the prophets are a part, a concern which Anthony F. C. Wallace makes clear in his now-famous essay, when he defines a "revitalization movement" as "a deliberate, organized, conscious effort by members of a society to construct a more satisfying culture".[1]

Beginning with Ralph Linton's essay on "nativistic movement"[2] there has been a continuing effort to classify these cults in terms of their beliefs and goals, as well as numerous attempts to define their causes. There have, of course, been many studies of individual movements, and these often take their departure from the kinds of theoretical analyses just mentioned. On the whole the same conditions persist in all these studies which led Jarvie to protest, with specific reference to theories of Cargo cults, that the prophetic leader himself has been unjustifiably neglected.[3]

Now it must be acknowledged that there are good reasons for these two tendencies, for real stumbling-blocks to the comparison of prophets arise from at least three sources. The first has to do with the nature of the given group's cultural adjustment. There are obvious and striking differences, say, between stone age, tribal men of aboriginal New Guinea or North America and iron age, urban men of the ancient Near East, which complicate the task of comparison. And these differences do not stop with the material culture, but extend to world-views as well. One can think of the Judeo-Christian "historical" tradition as opposed to native mythological traditions and observe that persons who write about prophets tend to come out of the former and spend time discussing the "irrationality" of the latter. A second and closely related stumbling-block involves the content of the prophecies themselves, which in all cases is culturally conditioned. Separate movements may share a general hope for the eventual appearance or return of some valued person or thing, but to what extent are the specific objects of hope (e.g., Jesus, the buffalo, the ancestors bringing cargo) comparable? Finally, there is a real danger that the investigator will fall prey to ethnocentricity and evaluate more highly what to him is more familiar or intelligible or "rational".

The difficulty of overcoming these barriers may be seen by glancing briefly at several attempts to do so. J. Lindblom, for example, approaches his study of ancient Israelite prophecy on the assumption that prophecy is a universal human phenomenon.[4] Early in the book he discusses extra-Israelite prophets and suggests what he considers to be the three defining characteristics of prophecy in general, namely that the prophet is a person who is conscious of having received a special call from his god, who has had revelatory experiences, and who proclaims to the people the message received through revelation. He then discusses the OT materials with reference to these characteristics. But the extra-Israelite prophets are not again brought into the discussion for purposes of comparison, and it is clear that one of Lindblom's main interests, to which he devotes the last third of the book, is the specific theological content of the ancient Israelite prophetic messages.

James Mooney's classic study of the Ghost Dance of 1890 is

another case in point. Mooney was not satisfied simply to describe the origin and development of this one prophetic movement, but attempted to set it in the context of a number of others which he took to be similar in character. Thus the first eight chapters of his book are devoted to descriptions of prophetic activity among various North American Indian groups, beginning with the Pueblo Revolt of 1680 and culminating with John Slocum and the Shakers of Puget Sound in the late nineteenth century. In addition a later chapter is devoted to "parallels in other systems", and discusses examples of such activity from the biblical period, Islam, and Christian sects and movements from the Middle Ages to the nineteenth century. Mooney does not elaborate any theoretical structure in terms of which he makes his comparisons, but one can find occasional statements that indicate he was using two general criteria in the selection of his materials. The first was the notion that messianic doctrines, wherever they are found, "are essentially the same and have their origin in a hope and longing common to all humanity".[5] The second is a list of traits – inspiration via dreams, dancing, ecstasy, and trance – which are taken to "have formed a part of every great religious development of which we have knowledge from the beginning of history".[6] Because of its scope, Mooney's study is important and interesting, but it is more a listing of movements than a systematic comparison. It avoids the stumbling-blocks mentioned above by not acknowledging their presence, and throws little theoretical light on the nature of the prophetic process.

It is clear that the effort to compare prophecy cross-culturally would be greatly facilitated if one could arrive at some basis for comparison that was as much as possible free from culturally-conditioned content. With this in mind I want to propose a model of how the prophetic process works, apply this model to the discussion of two specific prophets, Jeremiah and Handsome Lake, and then suggest several implications that seem to me to follow from this approach to prophecy. The claim I wish to make is that although the specific *content* of their respective messages is culturally conditioned and, therefore, quite dissimilar, the prophetic *activity* of the two conforms to the same general pattern.

Before introducing the model itself, a word seems in order regarding its genesis. My own training has been in biblical studies, and my primary interest OT prophecy. I gradually became aware of and interested in what appeared to be prophetic movements among American Indians, and a post-doctoral fellowship which allowed me to spend a year studying anthropology afforded the opportunity for an extensive investigation of one such, the Ghost Dance of 1890. Though a formal cross-cultural comparison was not part of my original intention, it eventually became evident that the Ghost Dance as well as other prophetic movements and figures that I studied had important features in common with OT prophecy. Reflection on this fact led to the development of the model, which I first proposed in a study of the Ghost Dance.[7] I view the model, then, as the natural outgrowth of my study of Israelite and non-Israelite prophetic movements and of the important interpretative literature that has been generated by the scholarly investigation of both.

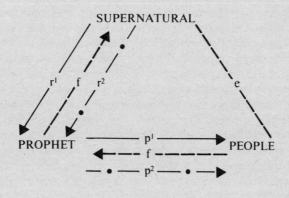

Fig. 1

Figure 1 states in the form of a diagram a way of understanding the nature of the prophetic process. The basic components of this model are two: a set of three actors and a pattern of interrelationships among them involving revelation (r), proclamation (p), feedback (f), and expectations of confirmation (e).

The focus on interrelationships that is evident here calls for some enlargement of traditional notions concerning a prophet's authority. Since the prophet functions as the messenger of the god, it seems justifiable to view his revelatory experiences as the primary source of his authority. In all instances of which I am aware it is simply assumed that a person who is truly functioning as a prophet has been the recipient of some such communication. These experiences are essentially private, and form the theological justification for his activity. They are also inevitably culturally-conditioned, since both his perception and later articulation of them will be affected by the cultural and historical context in which he stands. In addition to this, however, there is a more public aspect of a prophet's authority which displays itself in various reactions to his message by the people to whom it is addressed. Since the act of prophecy must necessarily take place in a social context, these reactions are both inevitable and of critical importance. For the prophet seeks to move his audience to action, and his hearers may be said to attribute authority to him in so far as they acknowledge and are prepared to act upon the "truth" of his formulation. In their response the hearers in effect judge the cultural "competence" of the prophet by deciding whether or not his message makes sense in the context of their cultural and religious traditions and is relevant to the current socio-political situation. As Peter Worsley has put it, "Charisma is thus a function of recognition; the prophet without honor cannot be a charismatic prophet."[8] We will return to this point below.

Though most of the prophet's audience will be members of his own cultural community, we can expect that they will not all be of one mind in their evaluation of his message. But whether individuals accept, reject, or are indifferent to it, they will react to the prophet in some fashion, and it is this "feedback" and the prophet's response to it that defines the dynamic interrelationship between actors that is central to the model. Similarly, the prophet will assess his own message against his perception of the events going on around him and the feedback he gets from his audience. Since in his understanding the message he delivers is not strictly his own but is revealed to him by the god, we also need to assume the possibility of feedback from the prophet to god and an eventual new revelation either confirming or altering the original message.

Operating on the basis of this model, we can now list in a more systematic way the component elements that we would expect to find in any given example of the prophetic process. The minimum number of elements necessary for the operation and identification of the process are three: 1. The prophet's revelation. 2. A proclamation based on that revelation, which will have the following general characteristic: though it will inevitably contain innovative features, the message will nonetheless "make sense" in the light of the cultural traditions of the prophet and his audience and the current social and historical situation in which they find themselves.[9] 3. An audience to whom the proclamation is addressed and whose reactions to it – positive, negative, or indifferent – will be determined in large part by how well the message is perceived to meet the criterion suggested above. Additional components (prophetic feedback to the source of revelation; additional revelations; additional messages; certain experiences, here labelled "expectations of confirmation", which tend to confirm independently the god-given task of the prophet and strengthen the conviction of his authenticity) are possible, in fact even probable, although our ability to discover them will depend largely on the amount of data extant for any given instance of prophecy. Sometimes a fourth "actor", in the form of one or more disciples who serve as intermediaries between the prophet and his audience, may be added to the basic model sketched in Figure 1.

Because a prophet speaks in a concrete historical situation and elicits a response from his audience partly on the basis of their judgements concerning what he says about it, it is necessary to preface the discussion of our two prophets with a brief sketch of the contexts within which they operated. The known public activity of the prophet Jeremiah spans approximately the last forty years of the existence of the Palestinian state of Judah (626–586 B.C.E.). For the century prior to this period Judah had been an Assyrian vassal state, but by the time Jeremiah appeared on the scene the power of the Assyrians had begun to wane, particularly in the outlying regions of their empire. Under King Josiah (640–609 B.C.E.) Judah began to reassert her independence. Her political influence was extended northward into the Assyrian provinces of Samaria and Galilee, and accompanying this rebellion there was a major reform of the Yahweh cult. Based on an old lawbook found during the remodelling of the Temple in 622, this reform sought to reassert the traditional form of the covenant relationship between Yahweh and his people.

But though independent, Judah's geographical position placed her in the middle of an international struggle for power that made her situation precarious. Revolts in both Egypt and Babylon had contributed to the weakening of the Assyrian empire, but as the pressure on the Assyrians by Medes and Babylonians became more intense (614–610), Egypt, hopeful of preserving a buffer state between herself and these new threatening powers, came to the aid of her old enemy and joined Assyria in an abortive attempt to recapture the city of Haran near the headwaters of the Euphrates. It was while he was on his way to this rendezvous in 609 that Pharaoh Necho met and killed Josiah in battle, and on his return from the Euphrates three months later deposed Josiah's successor and placed a Judean of his own choice, Jehoiakim, on the throne in Jerusalem. Four years later in 605 the Babylonian king Nebuchadnezzar decisively defeated the Egyptian army at Carchemish on the Euphrates, and Judah again found herself squarely between two opposing powers.

As one might expect, there was considerable factionalism in Judah over how best to respond to this situation. During his reign, Jehoiakim and his supporters among the princes adhered to a pro-Egypt policy and came into open conflict with Jeremiah.[10] The king eventually revolted against Nebuchadnezzar, and the result of this action was the capture of Jerusalem and the deportation of persons and property to Babylon in the year 597. Under Zedekiah, the last king of Judah, the same party dispute continued. The majority of the princes seemed to have been solidly pro-Egyptian, while the proclamations of Jeremiah became explicitly pro-Babylonian in the sense that he interpreted Nebuchadnezzar's conquest of Jerusalem as Yahweh's will and instructed the people to be obedient to their Babylonian overlord (cf. Jer. 27—29). The king wavered, but ultimately threw in with the former group. Judah revolted again, and Jerusalem was again besieged and captured. More of the population was exiled, and the city itself was destroyed and the Temple of Yahweh burned. The prophet elected to stay in Judah, but shortly was carried away to Egypt against his will by a group of fleeing Judeans (cf. Jer. 37—44).

This series of events presented the participants in them with a complex political and theological problem. Decisions were required concerning concrete and appropriate political and military actions, and in this critical time some looked to the religious traditions of the people for guidance. But prophets differed (cf. Jer. 28), and no single answer satisfactory to all emerged.

Turning now to the New World, the Seneca tribe of North American Indians to which the prophet Handsome Lake belonged had been a member of the famed Iroquois League, a closely knit confederation of tribes whose origin predates the arrival of Columbus. During much of the eighteenth century, this confederation was able, through a system of playing off the British against the French, both to maintain its territory and security and benefit from the material goods of European culture. But all that ended during the Revolution, which split the confederacy. Neutrality was abandoned, and most of the Iroquois gave their loyalty to the British. The ultimate result was that nearly all of their villages from the Mohawk River to the Ohio country were destroyed and they were cut off from their allies to the west, who established their own confederacy separate from the Iroquois.

The reservation system which was gradually imposed upon the Iroquois during the last decades of the century created what Wallace calls "slums in the wilderness, where no traditional Indian culture could long survive and where only the least useful aspects of white culture could easily penetrate".[11] The Cornplanter grant on the Allegheny River in northern Pennsylvania was somewhat unique among the reservations because of its relative isolation from white settlement. Though the influences of European material culture were considerable, many of the old social and political customs survived and the annual cycle of traditional religious ceremonials was still observed. It was there that Handsome Lake, Cornplanter's half-brother, resided. Of course, such isolation could only be relative, and the social pathologies that had been making inroads among the Iroquois for years were found also in Cornplanter's town. Drinking was a particularly serious problem.[12]

As in the case of Judah in Jeremiah's day, there was no unanimity of opinion among the Iroquois as to how to confront the problems inherent in their historical and cultural situation. Each reservation had its factions, the progressives "advocating the assimilation of white culture" and the conservatives "the preservation of Indian ways".[13] Cornplanter may be reckoned with the former group, and by the time of Handsome Lake's vision his village had already come under the influence of Quaker missionaries. These men were non-dogmatic in their approach to religion, and chose to concentrate on offering positive assistance to the Cornplanter Seneca in such practical areas as farming, carpentry, and education. By May of 1799 they had also persuaded the council to ban the use of whiskey in the village.[14]

The model outlined above assumes that for the prophetic process to occur there is required, first of all, a set of three actors designated the supernatural, the prophet, and the people. In the pages that follow we will be dealing with two such sets. The prophets are Jeremiah, a Judean of the late seventh and early sixth centuries B.C.E., and Handsome Lake, a Seneca who lived in the late eighteenth and early nineteenth centuries C.E. Jeremiah addressed his message to Judeans, primarily the inhabitants of the royal city of Jerusalem. Handsome Lake's message was directed to the Seneca of Cornplanter's band and, subsequently, other groups of Iroquois. The supernatural powers from whom each received his revelation were those familiar to the people: Yahweh, the ancestral God of Israel, and the Iroquois Creator.

The second basic component of the prophetic process is a pattern of interrelationships among these actors. I have termed the modes of this interaction revelation, proclamation, expectations of confirmation and feedback. The latter is especially important, since it allows us to understand what has sometimes been conceived of as a one-way informational flow as a dynamic, two-way process. For the sake of brevity the following discussion will centre mainly on two sequences of action involving revelation, proclamation and feedback.

The prophetic process involves what we might call a *revelation-feedback-revelation sequence*. The Book of Jeremiah opens with an account of an experience that Jeremiah understood to be a revelation from Yahweh commissioning him to be a prophet (1:4–10). Both from the style in which the various utterances of the prophet are framed and reports of other visionary or auditory experiences,[15] it seems clear that Jeremiah continued to receive revelations. But this communication with Yahweh was not all one-way. In the call vision itself Jeremiah is pictured as protesting against the role that was being put upon him (1:6), and these protests continued in a series of six "laments" or "complaints" in which he lashed out against his enemies,[16] complained about the burdens of his office (20:7–9, 14–18), and accused Yahweh himself of acting unfaithfully (15:18; 20:7–9).

It is important to point out that one of the factors in the mutual hostility between Jeremiah and some of his hearers was the question of the validity of his revelation and the message derived from it. Because he understood it to be part of what had been revealed to him, Jeremiah continually announced that disaster would befall the nation of Judah (cf. 1:10, 13–19; 17:16). But the people, who in any case would not have been overjoyed at such a message, at some point began to subject him to intense ridicule because the threatened calamity had failed to occur (17:15; 20:7f.). The prophet also seems to have had his doubts about the revelation (15:18; 20:7), and these formed one element in his feedback to Yahweh.

The book also provides us with two examples of Yahweh's rejoinder to the prophet's feedback (12:5f.; 15:19–23), and these can be considered "additional revelations" which in effect confirmed the prophet's original message. By implication we can assume that a similar feedback-response sequence lies behind that portion of the Hananiah episode (chapter 28) in which Jeremiah was temporarily unable to dispute the message of his opponent, but "sometime later" returned to condemn him as a liar. Further, it seems necessary to assume that, given the nature of prophecy, any alteration in message would be understood by the prophet to be grounded in an additional revelation from god, and therefore in so far as the announcement of a "new covenant" (31:31–4) and other passages of a more "positive" tone (e.g., 32:1–15) can be taken to reflect a genuine element of Jeremiah's message, they also imply further revelations.

The Gaiwiio ("Good Message"), a record of Handsome Lake's teachings which is still in use among followers of the "Longhouse way",[17] begins by describing a "time of troubles" in Cornplanter village. The scene is at first community-wide. A party of Indians had just returned from Pittsburg, where they had traded skins and game for whiskey. A wild drinking party followed in which village life was disrupted and some families moved away for safety. The focus then shifts to a single sick man, who was held in the grip of "some strong power" and feared that he might die. Realizing that the cause of his illness was whiskey, he resolved never to use it again. Afraid that he would not have the strength to do this, he prayed to the "Great Ruler" and began to be confident that his prayer had been heard and he would live. The sick man was Handsome Lake.[18]

On 17 June, 1799, the sick man appeared to die. His body was prepared for burial and relatives summoned, but he revived and reported he had had a vision of three messengers who had been sent to reveal to him the Creator's will and instruct him to carry it to the people. The vision also contained a threat, for Handsome Lake was shown the steaming grave of a man who had formerly been commissioned "to proclaim that message to the world", but had "refused to obey". On 7 August of the same year the prophet received his second revelation in which he was guided on a journey through heaven and hell and given moral instruction. A third revelation occurred on 5 February, 1800. Each of these visions was reported and discussed in a council of the people.

Several passages in the Gaiwiio make it clear that Handsome Lake expected to receive further revelations. In his initial vision the three messengers promised, "We shall continually reveal things unto you", and this promise was repeated in 1809 when in the midst of a personal crisis the messengers came to the prophet and said, "We understand your thoughts. We will visit you more frequently and converse with you."[19] Although the present form of the Gaiwiio makes it difficult to date specific revelations, there is some internal evidence of such a continuing sequence. Most conspicuous are the place names. The Gaiwiio specifically sets the initial vision in Cornplanter's village, but subsequent sections are said to derive from Cold Spring, Tonawanda, and Onondaga (all in New York).[20] These localities correspond to known periods of the prophet's activity. Furthermore, there are at least four sections of the Code that Wallace links to specific, dateable events: a derogatory reference to Chief Red Jacket arising out of a dispute over the sale of reservation land in 1801, a prophecy intended to discourage Iroquois participation in the "war in the west" (1811), and a composite section mentioning the people's reviling of Handsome Lake and his meeting with the Spirit of the Corn which seems to mirror events that took place in the years 1809 and 1815.[21] The final sections of the Code deal with the revelations and events immediately preceding the prophet's death, which occurred on 10 August, 1815, at Onondaga.[22] It is clear that these revelations did not simply repeat what had gone before. They arose out of Handsome Lake's attempt to deal with new situations, and were doubtless seen by him to be divine responses to his own quest for a solution.

The prophetic process involves as well a *proclamation-feedback-proclamation sequence*. Throughout his long career Jeremiah seems to have proclaimed a fairly consistent message, viz., that because of their actions and the "falsehood" that pervaded their existence the people were standing on the brink of a great national catastrophe. This message evoked both positive and negative responses from the people, though judging from the material available to us, the latter predominated. The negative feedback was sometimes stated in terms of derision because the destruction he proclaimed had not yet come to pass (17:15; 20:7f.). In addition there are reports that he was at various times of his life threatened (11:18–23; 18:18, 22; 20:10), put in the stocks and beaten (20:1–6; cf. 29:26–8), brought to trial on a trumped-up charge (26:7–19), thrown into an abandoned cistern in hopes that he would die (38:1–6), charged with treason (37:13f.; 38:1–4), and imprisoned (32:2f.; 37:15f., 20f.).

A further negative response to his proclamation can be seen in the numerous references to prophetic opponents whose message of "peace" contradicted that of Jeremiah (cf. 6:9–15; 23:9–40). A classic example because of its richness in narrative detail is the conflict with the prophet Hananiah recounted in chapter 28. We also have references to persons simply refusing to obey instructions conveyed to them by Jeremiah as the will of Yahweh (43:1–7; 44:15–

19). On the other hand, there are instances of positive feedback. There were individuals and groups which supported the prophet,[23] as well as occasions on which he was sought out by someone who wished to learn Yahweh's will for the current situation.[24]

I have already suggested that the response of the people to a prophet will depend largely upon whether they perceive his message to be in continuity with their cultural and religious traditions and relevant to the current sociopolitical situation. But this is a rather flexible criterion, and not likely to lead to complete unanimity of opinion. It puts a tremendous burden upon the hearers, each of whom will be tempted to view the matter in terms of his own self-interests. It is evident that both Jeremiah and Hananiah had a following, and that the supporters of each could find some legitimate grounds for believing that their man's message was faithful to the tradition and relevant to the situation. I have dealt specifically with this problem in another place, and will not repeat that discussion here.[25] It is sufficient for our present purposes to point out the intensity and significance of this feedback from the people to the prophet and suggest the mechanism by which it works.

As to whether the content of Jeremiah's message was affected by this feedback, the data are not so clear. In the Hananiah episode we have reference to a specific occasion on which the prophet was at least temporarily blocked and forced to retreat for some reconsideration and/or renewal of his message (28:11–16). Taken in conjunction with other passages in which he expresses doubts about his revelation (15:18; 20:7), it would seem reasonable to conclude that the intensity of the negative feedback Jeremiah experienced from time to time caused him to reconsider both the content of what he said and his own continuance in the prophetic office (cf. 20:9). Beyond that, the passages of more positive tone referred to above may indicate a response to a changing historical situation (looking beyond the destruction of Judah and Jerusalem) and mark the beginning of a substantive change in the prophet's long-standing proclamation of doom.

A summary of Handsome Lake's proclamation to the Iroquois has come down to us in the Gaiwiio. This narrative begins with an account of an episode of drunkenness and destruction in Cornplanter's village and of the prophet's sickness, death, and resurrection. It is in connection with the latter experience that the main themes of Handsome Lake's proclamation assert themselves, for the messengers revealed to him the four great wrongs by which "men spoil the laws the Great Ruler has made and thereby make him angry": drinking whiskey, using witchcraft, using "compelling charms", and practising abortion. In the remaining sections considerable space is given to positive commands relating to social behaviour (gossip, drunkenness, sharing, mourning customs, etc.), family life (the care of children, husband-wife relationships, the care of elders), and religion (the medicine societies were ordered to disband, but a number of the traditional ceremonies are specifically sanctioned and regulated). In addition the Code deals in several places with the relationship between Indians and whites (agriculture, schooling, and the Creator's protection of his people against extermination by the whites) and with the status of the prophet (disbelief is said to be due to the operation of an evil spirit, and will be punished). A number of these themes are reinforced in the sections recounting the second revelation (the "sky journey"), where Handsome Lake witnessed the suffering of a variety of sinners (drunkard, wife-beater, gambler, etc.) in the house of the "punisher". Finally, there is reference to the apocalyptic themes of the sin of the world and the world's end and renewal.

Wallace understands the preaching of Handsome Lake to fall into two distinct phases. The first, covering the years 1799 to 1801, was characterized by an "apocalyptic gospel" in which the people were summoned to repentance and the recurring themes were world destruction, sin, and salvation. The second phase began in 1801 and featured a "social gospel" in which the main values that were stressed were "temperance, peace and unity, land retention, acculturation, and a revised domestic morality".[26] As in the case of Jeremiah the response to this message was mixed. In the early years he was able to exercise both political and religious power, and the council at Buffalo Creek in 1801 prohibited the use of liquor and appointed him "High Priest, and principal Sachem in all things Civil and Religious". Over the next few years, however, his political influence declined. In 1807 the Iroquois confederacy was reorganized and the great council fire established at Buffalo Creek, where one of the prophet's chief rivals, Red Jacket, was influential. Handsome Lake and Cornplanter also quarrelled, and factions developed in the Allegany band, causing the prophet to move out and locate first at Cold Spring and later at Tonawanda. But his religious influence remained strong. He made an annual circuit of visitations to other reservations preaching his gospel and winning converts.[27] As Wallace describes it, "These conversions were not casual matters. The Indians traversed the same mystic path to Gaiwiio as white converts to Christianity; the converts retained an intense devotion to the prophet who gave them strength to achieve salvation. One of the Onondagas, when asked why they did not leave their drunken habits before, since they were often urged to do it, and saw the ruinous consequences of such conduct, replied, they had no power; but when the Great Spirit forbade such conduct by their prophet, he gave them the power to comply with their request."[28]

What one notices about the Gaiwiio is how directly it spoke to the situation that plagued the Iroquois of Handsome Lake's day. Addressing a people debauched and demoralized by contact with white culture and the loss of their own traditional ways, the Gaiwiio accused them of wrongdoing, laying heavy stress on evils disruptive of harmonious community life (strong drink, witchcraft, charms, and abortion).[29] In its commandments great emphasis was placed on the strengthening of family relationships and the regulation of social behaviour. In response to the growing influence of white culture there was explicit approval of farming, house-building, animal husbandry, and, to a limited extent, education "in English schools".[30]

In real life parts of this message evoked a negative response and caused the prophet trouble, particularly his determined attacks against witchcraft and supposed witch-inspired conspiracies. Reaction to the execution of one witch in 1809 caused him to have to leave Cold Spring, a situation reflected in the Gaiwiio: "Now it was that when the people reviled me, the proclaimer of the prophecy, the impression came to me that it would be well to depart and go to Tonawanda. In that place I had relatives and friends and thought that my bones might find a resting place there."[31] Other sections which mirror responses to feedback in specific situations have been mentioned above.

The Gaiwiio spoke to the current situation, advocating such important cultural innovations as the involvement of men in farm labour, limited acceptance of white education, and the dissolution of the totem animal societies. But for all that, the Gaiwiio "made sense" in the light of the traditions of the past. Social solidarity was stressed in the ethical commandments of the Code, and in particular the old religious values and ceremonies were for the most part retained. Its major new religious concept, the notion of judgement and afterlife in heaven or hell, was compatible with the old beliefs and was introduced "to insure the dedication of the people to conservative ritual". Handsome Lake "was in his own eyes as the messenger of God, necessarily the defender of the faith".[32] As Parker puts it, "Handsome Lake sought to destroy the ancient folk-ways of the people and to substitute a new system, *built of course upon the framework of the old.*"[33] Eventually, a myth even developed to account for the origin of the conditions that made the Gaiwiio necessary and fix its place in the overall order of things.

The position taken in this paper is that feedback from the people to the prophet is important both because of its potential for helping to shape the latter's message and because their acceptance forms one of the bases of his prophetic authority. That the message of Handsome Lake gained such wide acceptance among the Iroquois in his own day would seem to be due largely to the skill with which he utilized the old traditions of the people in addressing himself to the crucial problems of the present. And when after his death (1815) some of the traditional Iroquois leaders sought a way to counter the threats of both sectarian Christian and disruptive nativists, they found it convenient to call upon the memory of Handsome Lake in attempting to define the form and spirit of the old religion. At the religious council at Tonawanda in the summer of 1818 John Sky repeated a version of Handsome Lake's teaching and a minor prophet recounted a vision of confirming it. Similar incidents occurred over the next two decades, and by the 1840s the text of the Code, which continues to this day to be an important force in Iroquois life, was fixed.

In discussing specific instances of prophecy we are always dependent upon the vicissitudes of historical reporting for our information. This is especially evident in the case of the final interactive element of the model, *expectations of confirmation.* We are dealing here largely with beliefs based upon circulating reports of individual experiences of a "supernatural" character, and such pious tales easily escape the attention of the chroniclers of prophetic movements. Nevertheless, enough examples are available to suggest that this element was of importance in the people's response to a prophet. Faith in Wovoka, the prophet of the Ghost Dance of 1890, was certainly enhanced by Indians returning from visits to his camp with tales of how he could control the weather and miraculously "shorten" the homeward journey of those who made the long trip from the northern Plains to western Nevada to visit him.[34] With respect to Handsome Lake the same dynamics can be seen at work in the Onondagas crediting the Great Spirit with giving them the power to give up alcohol and follow the Gaiwiio, as well as in the visions of other prophets confirming his message.

If it is difficult to find such clear examples as this in Jeremiah (20:7–8 and 44:16–19 rather seem to echo disconfirming experiences), that is perhaps because the book as we have it is preoccupied with the negative reactions of Jeremiah's audience to him.

It seems fair to conclude on the basis of the foregoing summary of evidence that the model which I have proposed for understanding the nature of the prophetic process "works" cross-culturally. That is to say, it provides us with categories in terms of which to compare the activity of two such culturally disparate holy men as Jeremiah and Handsome Lake in a fashion not unduly prejudiced by the obvious differences in their respective messages. This is an important conclusion in several respects. In the first place it has been pointed out above that the processes of interaction which lie at the heart of the prophetic act have for the most part not been given their due by students of prophetic movements. Moreover, it would seem that adopting this view of prophecy enables us to put into satisfactory perspective three interrelated problems which are important for any attempt to understand prophecy: the nature of the situation in which the prophet operates, the nature of prophetic authority, and the problem of how the content of a prophet's proclamation relates to the cultural tradition in which he stands.

The prophetic process has its locus in a specific situation. This means that any discussion of a prophet's activity will need to be informed by details of the cultural context and historical moment in which he operated. The question is whether in comparing situations which gave rise to prophecy one can say anything beyond the widely recognized fact that they are invariably times of "crisis". Let me briefly suggest, with the aid of concepts borrowed from Kenelm Burridge and Clifford Geertz, that it is possible to understand these situations more fully.

Burridge's view of the prophetic situation derives from his notion that religion is "the redemptive process indicated by the activities, moral rules, and assumptions about power which, pertinent to the moral order and taken on faith, not only enable a people to perceive the truth of things, but guarantee that they are indeed perceiving the truth of things".[35] Religion thus establishes a prestige system in which the criteria of one's integrity within the social order are well known and consistent with everyday experience. The crisis of the prophetic situation resides specifically in the fact that events have taken place (usually involving contact with another culture) which have posed a serious challenge to these assumptions. The result is that the experience of a loss of prestige and integrity and the need for regeneration are widely felt among the populace. In a similar fashion Geertz speaks of a religious system as a cluster of sacred symbols woven into an ordered whole which supports a certain view of morality "by picturing a world in which such conduct is only common sense".[36] Religion creates a synthesis of ethos (the moral and aesthetic tone of a culture) and world view (a culture's picture of the way things are in sheer actuality). Either of these elements taken by itself "is arbitrary, but taken together they form a gestalt with a peculiar kind of inevitability".[37] Above all, such symbolic activities are "attempts to provide orientation for an organism which cannot live in a world it is unable to understand."[38] The prophetic situation, then, is one in which the basic religio-cultural understanding has been undermined. In what did the integrity of the Seneca male reside, now that the game animals were depleted and he could no longer go to war? To be able to subsist, more emphasis had to be put on farming, but that was woman's work! And what could be more damaging to the system of beliefs about Yahweh's election and protection of his people Israel than the death of "good king Josiah" and the first Babylonian conquest of Jerusalem (597 B.C.E.) and exiling of its inhabitants? In these situations men found chaos breaking in upon them, but heard as well prophets like Jeremiah and Handsome Lake proclaiming an interpretation which promised a new order.

This leads to a second problem, viz. how one is to understand the basis or source of a prophet's authority. My main concern here has been to avoid a one-way interpretation of the prophet's activity, that is to say, an interpretation of the power of the prophet over others which dwells too exclusively on the presumed divine source of his message. The divine revelation which the prophet claims is, of course, important to his understanding of himself (cf. Amos 3:8), and can be used to justify his utterances (Jer. 26:12–15) and condemn his opponents (Jer. 28:15–16). It is also an important element in the people's understanding of a prophet. But despite this fact the prophet's exercise of his role cannot be effective unless his message is met with a positive response on the part of at least some of his hearers.

Thus there are two aspects to the prophet's authority. On the one hand, the prophet makes the claim that the deity has authorized the proclamation of a certain message. The basis of this claim is usually a religious experience which is private and therefore essentially intangible and unverifiable by the members of his audience, who nevertheless assume that a genuine prophet will have had such an experience. I wish to be emphatic about this, since the "call" of a deity is an absolutely crucial element in the constitution of a given occurrence of prophecy, not only in the OT but in other cultures as well. On the other hand, the prophet cannot be effective, cannot function as a prophet, unless the people acknowledge his claim to authority by their reaction to his words, and the social reality of prophecy depends upon this act. The brute fact behind the words of Peter Worsley quoted above is that the members of the prophet's audience are free to choose whom they will follow. Burke Long has summarized the matter in this way:

> The authority of a prophet was a vulnerable, shifting social reality – closely tied to acceptance and belief. It was supported by concrete deeds of power . . . But the authority rested upon acceptance of those appeals.[39]

To speak of authority in terms of acceptance is to acknowledge that, from the point of view of the hearers, a particular instance of prophecy will be deemed "authoritative" on the basis of certain tangible marks. One such mark is the prophet's ability to clarify and articulate what the people who follow him have themselves begun to feel about their particular situation. His utterances are experienced as having explanatory power. Burridge in fact sees the task of the prophet as one of organizing and articulating a new set of assumptions which suggest a way of making sense out of the chaos of the present situation. In doing so he concentrates in himself the people's own probings, and his revelation usually "echoes the theorizing and experimentation that has gone before".[40] The prophet is thus a transitional figure in a redemptive process the goal of which is the regeneration of the people as a group, i.e., the creation of new assumptions about power in the broad sense, a new politico-economic framework, a new mode of measuring man, new criteria of integrity, a new community. The people choose their prophets, that is they attribute authority to them, because they perceive in their proclamation continuity with the cultural traditions sufficient to make what they say intelligible and at the same time innovations sufficient to offer the possibility of a new interpretation that will bring order out of chaos. Thus, a second and closely related mark of a prophet's authority is the effectiveness, real or imagined, which seems to characterize his activities. This effectiveness is perhaps most often experienced in the form of rhetorical skill (to his followers the prophet's message "makes sense" out of the current crisis situation), but marvellous acts, including instances of fulfilled prophecy, may also play a role. Such seemingly supernatural occurrences help to confirm the authenticity of the prophet. They are accounted for in the model under the rubric "expectations of confirmation".

From the point of view of audience reaction, then, the general criterion for the attribution of authority to a prophet might be expressed as "perceived effectiveness". The hearers do not by their act of attributing authority to a prophet confer his powers on him, since, from one point of view, the claim to supernatural designation means that he already has or is perceived to have these powers. What they do, in effect, is confirm him in his role. Their affirmative response, necessary for his exercise of that role, is an act of commitment based on their recognition of that power. It must be stressed, however, that while some positive response to his message appears to be necessary for the operation of prophecy, large numbers are not. Crenshaw[41] has shown with respect to the OT prophets that conflict with perhaps the great majority of those who heard them (even other prophets) was "inevitable" and that on the whole they had little impact upon their contemporaries. That they had some support, however, is shown both by references to specific instances (Isaiah's mention of his disciples, 8:16; the aid Jeremiah received from various members of the house of Shaphan, 26:4, chap. 36) and by the very fact that their utterances were preserved, collected, and eventually committed to writing.

Perhaps one of the most striking examples of this role of the people is the case of Yali, a native leader in post-World War II New Guinea. Though he made no supernatural claims for himself, his audience began to attribute prophetic authority to him, in effect making him a prophet even in the absence of any claims to revelatory experience. Without their reaction he would neither have claimed to be nor functioned as a prophet. Since prophecy is always situation-bound and public, private revelation alone is insufficient to establish its authority.

This leads, finally, to the problem of how much "old" and how much "new" we might expect to find in a prophet's message. There can, of course, be no neat formula. Clearly, the message must have enough recognizable roots in the traditional but now threatened cultural synthesis for it to be understood and acceptable. In Burridge's scheme the millennial prophet is central to a process by which a people moves from a time when the "old rules" of the society remained intact, through an interim time of "no rules", and to a final synthesis of a set of "new rules".[42] Thus a consistent theme in Handsome Lake's preaching was condemnation of the individual autonomy and glorification that had been characteristic of the old Iroquois way, lately fallen into the chaos of social pathology, while advocating in its place restraint in social affairs. Elizabeth Tooker has suggested that what the prophet was trying to do was "to introduce a value system ... consistent with the economic system that was also introduced at the same time".[43] With the collapse of the old hunting-trading system the Iroquois were forced into more intensive agriculture, but plough agriculture is a man's work and the yearly agricultural schedule demands a stable social order. Therefore, the values he selected emphasized communal order over individual gratification. If these values were similar to those of the white society, it was primarily because both were agrarian.

That the message of the OT prophets arises out of and is in dialogue with the religious traditions of their people is well-known. For his part Jeremiah stood within the old Exodus-election tradition of Judah (cf. for example, 2:1–8). His accusations against the people make it clear that from his viewpoint (i.e., that of a "pure" Yahwist; one wonders how many such there were among his compatriots) the present period was one of "no" rules, at least in the sense that the people had chosen to ignore important aspects of their covenant with Yahweh. Put differently, we might say that he was interpreting the fruits of a long process of acculturation in the land of Canaan as apostasy. Yet in the future he saw the institution of a "new covenant", one recognizable in terms of the old but operating on the basis of new assumptions about the nature of the relationship between Yahweh and Israel (31:31–4).

Almost inevitably when we look at a prophet we consider first the content of his proclamation, and having adopted this approach we are likely to be most impressed by his differences from all other prophets about whom we know. The argument of this paper has been that when we go beneath the level of content to that of process significant similarities begin to emerge. And having learned something about the underlying similarities of two specific prophets, Jeremiah and Handsome Lake, we have, I believe, gained at least some understanding of all other prophets as well.

NOTES

1 A. F. C. Wallace, "Revitalization Movements", *AA* 58 (1956) 264–81; see p. 265.
2 R. Linton, "Nativistic Movements", *AA* 45 (1943) 230–40.

Prophecy: The Problem of Cross-Cultural Comparison

3 I. C. Jarvie, "Theories of Cargo Cults: a Critical Analysis", *Oceania* 34 (1963) 1–31, 108–36; see p. 131.

4 Johannes Lindblom, *Prophecy in Ancient Israel* (Oxford: Blackwell, 1962).

5 James Mooney, "The Ghost-Dance Religion and the Sioux Outbreak of 1890", *Annual Report of the Bureau of American Ethnology* 14 (Washington: Government Printing Office, 1896) 657.

6 Mooney, "The Ghost Dance Religion", 928; see 719, 947.

7 Thomas W. Overholt, "The Ghost Dance of 1890 and the Nature of the Prophetic Process", *Ethnohistory* 21 (1974) 37–63.

8 Peter Worsley, *The Trumpet Shall Sound*, 2nd edn (New York: Schocken, 1968) xii.

9 Homer G. Barnett, *Innovation: The Basis of Cultural Change* (New York: McGraw-Hill, 1953) 181–266.

10 Cf. Jer. 26 and 36. In all of this Jeremiah, too, had his supporters in high places. Note particularly the references to members of the house of Shaphan in Jer. 26:24; 29:3; 36:10–13, 25; 40:5f.; 41:2.

11 Anthony F. C. Wallace, *The Death and Rebirth of the Seneca* (New York: Vintage, 1972) 184.

12 The followers of Handsome Lake recounted a legend of how the "evil one" enticed an unsuspecting young European to bring a bundle of "five things" (a flask of rum, a pack of playing cards, some coins, a violin, and a decaying leg bone) across the ocean to the Indians. This gift resulted in great misery and made necessary the "Good Message" or Gaiwiio. Cf. Arthur C. Parker, "The Code of Handsome Lake the Seneca Prophet", *New York State Museum Bulletin* 163 (Albany: Univ. of the State of New York Press, 1913) 16–19.

13 Wallace, *The Death and Rebirth of the Seneca*, 202.

14 Wallace, *The Death and Rebirth of the Seneca*, 221–36.

15 Jer. 1:11–12, 13–19; 13:1–11; 18:1–11; 19:1–15; 24:1–10.

16 Jer. 11:20; 12:1–4; 15:5; 17:18; 18:21–3.

17 Annemarie Shimony, *Conservatism among the Iroquois at the Six Nations Reserve*. Yale Univ. Publications in Anthropology 65 (New Haven: Department of Anthropology, 1961).

18 Parker, "The Code of Handsome Lake", 20–2.

19 Parker, "The Code of Handsome Lake", 25, 47.

20 Parker, "The Code of Handsome Lake", 20, 46f., 57, 60–2, 76–80.

21 Parker, "The Code of Handsome Lake", 68, 65f., 47.

22 Parker, "The Code of Handsome Lake", 76–80.

23 Jer. 26:16–19, 24; 36:13–19; 39:11–14; 40:1–6.

24 Jer. 21:1f.; 38:14–16; 42:1–3.

25 Thomas W. Overholt, *The Threat of Falsehood: A Study in the Theology of the Book of Jeremiah* (London: SCM, 1970).

26 Wallace, *The Death and Rebirth of the Seneca*, 278; cf. 239–302.

27 Wallace, *The Death and Rebirth of the Seneca*, 260f.; 286ff., 296ff.

28 Wallace, *The Death and Rebirth of the Seneca*, 301.
29 Parker, "The Code of Handsome Lake", 27–30.
30 Parker, "The Code of Handsome Lake", 38.
31 Parker, "The Code of Handsome Lake", 47.
32 Wallace, *The Death and Rebirth of the Seneca*, 318; cf. 251–4, 315–18.
33 Parker, "The Code of Handsome Lake", 114. Emphasis added.
34 Overholt, "The Ghost Dance of 1890", 47f.
35 Kenelm O. L. Burridge, *New Heaven, New Earth* (New York: Schocken, 1969) 6–7.
36 Clifford Geertz, *The Interpretation of Cultures* (New York: Basic Books, 1973) 129.
37 Geertz, *The Interpretation of Cultures*, 130.
38 Geertz, *The Interpretation of Cultures*, 140–1.
39 Burke O. Long, "Prophetic Authority as Social Reality", in *Canon and Authority*, ed. G. W. Coats *et al.* 3–20 (Philadelphia: Fortress, 1977) 19.
40 Burridge, *New Heaven, New Earth*, 111; cf. 11–14.
41 James L. Crenshaw, *Prophetic Conflict: Its Effects upon Israelite Religion* (BZAW 124; Berlin: de Gruyter, 1971).
42 Burridge, *New Heaven, New Earth*, 165–9.
43 Elizabeth Tooker, "On the New Religion of Handsome Lake", *Anthropological Quarterly* 41 (1968) 187–200; see p. 187.

5

*The Social Organization of Peasant Poverty in Biblical Israel**

BERNHARD LANG

Where the means of production are fragmented, usury centralizes monetary wealth. It does not change the mode of production, but clings on to it like a parasite and impoverishes it. It sucks it dry, emasculates it and forces reproduction to proceed under ever more pitiable conditions. Hence the popular hatred of usury, at its peak in the ancient world ... In Asiatic forms, usury can persist for a long while without leading to anything more than economic decay and political corruption. (Karl Marx, *Capital*, vol. 3, ch. 36)[1]

Amos, a prophet active in eighth-century B.C. northern Israel, remains an elusive figure. Possibly he tried to instigate a coup d'état against the king, Jeroboam, whom he knew to be unwilling or unable to carry through social reforms such as a general remission or reduction of peasant debt or a restriction of debt bondage. Like his younger contemporary, Hosea, he may have thought that a reunion of the two kingdoms, Israel and Judah, under the leadership of the Davidic dynasty would solve political and social problems. He enforced his programme – if that is the right word for it – not only by making it the explicit will of Yahweh, the God of the state, but also by announcing a military invasion of the Assyrians who would destroy the urban centres and thus "punish" the élite for its social crimes. Whether this prophet's activity had any impact on society we do not know. Possibly he left the country after having cursed the priest of Bethel who had denounced him at the royal court, as well as his wife whose fate as a city prostitute he angrily announced (Amos 7:17).

*First published in *Monotheism and the Prophetic Minority* by Bernhard Lang (1983) 114–27. In the interest of brevity the notes have been slightly abridged.

Though partly based on a statement made by an upper-class contemporary of Amos (i.e. priest Amaziah) and on comparative evidence,[2] this reading represents no more than an educated guess. Scholarly imagination is indispensable, yet a poor substitute for lacking sources and evidence not available.

Whereas the aim of Amos and the precise nature of his activity must remain a matter of conjecture, his literary legacy provides us with much evidence for the economic and social situation that obtained in his society.

Wealth and poverty, townsmen and peasants are contrasted with one another in a harsh manner.

> [Shame on] you who loll in beds inlaid with ivory
> and sprawl over your couches,
> feasting on lambs from the flock
> and fatted calves ...

reads chapter 6:4. And from chapter 5:11 we can guess at the source of the luxury:

> You levy taxes on the poor
> and extort a tribute of grain from them.

Whether one speaks of economic classes or social strata does not make any difference – the contrast cannot be overlooked, and the words of Amos made him famous as an early social critic if not as a people's tribune. It is, of course, much more difficult to analyse the background of the obvious class differences. How did such an economic stratification come about?

The older commentators did not see any problem here. For biblical Israel as well as for their own society they took poverty and wealth for granted – as facts that could not be altered. However, what could be changed was the conduct of the rich – and thus the prophet was understood. Egotistic exploitation was to give place to the patron's solidarity: the rich were to soften the harshness of poverty through well-directed gifts and thus to recreate some kind of social balance.

Another view, arguing from social history, was taken by the last generation of scholars and is still to be found in the standard literature. According to this view, the contrast between poor and rich is a Canaanite feature and belongs to the urban culture of ancient Palestine. The background of the prophetic protest – so it was argued – is provided by an egalitarian ideal which implies the basic economic equality of the whole Israelite peasant population.

But from the era of David and Solomon onwards there has been a progressive "Canaanization" of the economic system which created the situation attacked by Amos. The prophet launched his protest as a spokesman for the old partly nomadic, partly agrarian, ideology of brotherhood that knows of no classes: "égalité" implies "fraternité"! Egalitarian Israel versus Canaanite classes provided the key to almost everything in Israel's social development. Recently, however, it has become clear that things are not to be explained so easily, and that an originally classless and egalitarian society is rather more wishful thinking than characteristic of the earliest Israel. But even if some Canaanite influence in the formation of a stratified society is admitted, the "Canaanite vs. Israelite systems" approach never explained *how* the exploiting system actually worked.

Peasants and Landlords in Near-Eastern Economic History

For these reasons it seems more promising to proceed from agrarian societies as studied by social anthropology. Such "peasant societies" as they are called are usually characterized by the following three traits:[3]

1 A peasant is not a farmer or an agricultural entrepreneur but rather maintains a household. Instead of earning a profit, he wants to feed his family, which is the basic economic unit. As for biblical Israel I may add that we are dealing with a nuclear family consisting of parents and unmarried children; as is the rule with us the newly married couple resides neolocally – it builds its own house.[4]

2 Peasants do not form a complete and independent society; in fact, they are only one half of it, the other half being a propertied, educated and merchant élite often resident in towns and always monopolizing control of public affairs.

3 The ruling class makes permanent charges on the agricultural production. There are different titles to do so: the right to taxation may be placed in the hands of a lord who inherited a village as his patrimonial domain (*patrimonial system*); or a lord may be paid by peasants in return for the exercise of some ecclesiastical or civil office (*prebendal system*). A third system does not involve a general rule over and taxation of peasants but rather leaves this to free business in the market. In this case, the peasant may run into debt and become dependent on an urban money-lender or merchant –

or he may be forced to cultivate the soil of others on a share-cropping or tenant basis.

In the Near East, this last arrangement between peasantry and élite which may be christened the *mercantile system* has found a particular expression in what is called *rent capitalism*.[5] The urban propertied class skims off the largest possible portion of the agricultural produce as a regular income or "rent" claimed on the basis of liabilities or full urban ownership of land. As a rule, there are dyadic contracts between an urban landowner or merchant and individual peasants.

I will proceed to illustrate and elucidate several aspects of this general description.

The small peasant living on his plot does not produce for the market but for his family and himself (subsistence economy). Given the existing productive techniques, crop yields are determined by factors outside the control of the producer – principally by variations in rainfall. The climatically conditioned crop failures can be balanced more or less by keeping a few cattle. If no more than every fourth harvest fails, the present-day peasant of Iraq breaks even,[6] thus achieving a stability which, however, fluctuates on the edge of disaster. If crop failures occur more frequently (e.g. caused by locusts or several successive droughts) then the peasants have to make use of credit. Equally, illness, payment of the bride wealth, etc. may force them to incur debts. Taking a loan almost automatically leads to long-term or even permanent dependence because of the high interest rates – in antiquity as today. Interest at the rate of 40–60% per six months and 5–8% per month are quoted for Syria in the 1960s.[7] According to documents from the fifth century B.C., the Jews of Elephantine in Egypt were expected to pay 5% per month, unpaid interest being added to the capital, which equals at least an annual interest rate of 60%.[8] In one passage the Bible tells us with all desirable accuracy how a free peasant becomes more and more dependent on a creditor: Gen. 47:13–26. It is reported that in a time of famine the Egyptians had to convey everything to the Pharaoh – first their cattle, then their land and even themselves, so that they were in bondage, owing to the king 20% of their annual yield. It is known that this passage does not fit in with the Egyptian economic system; rather, it reflects how the poor Israelite peasant becomes dependent on a rich lord.[9]

As a rule, credit is taken from a rich townsman who often becomes the actual owner of the cultivated land. Thus ownership of land and labour are separated: whereas the agricultural production remains with the small family, the land is entirely or in part property of a landlord. Not always[10] but very often and typically, the landowner is a townsman so that the dualism of rich and poor corresponds to the country's dependence on the city. As an indebted peasant or small tenant the poor man is the landlord's bondsman and sometimes a kind of serf or even slave – especially when he has to render regular or occasional services in addition to the payment of rent.

> The rich lord it over the poor;
> the borrower becomes the lender's slave (or serf)

says Prov. 22:7.[11] While a serf is working, the creditor or landlord draws an income without actually working for it, enjoying the pleasant life of the leisure class.

The wish to lead such a life rests on the disdain for any physical work – compare the attitude of the patricians of classical Athens. People want to earn their living as great merchants, major civil servants or big landowners. Manual work is considered to be menial and degrading, and hence for the lower classes. Exemption from labour is the only true criterion of distinction: he who is at the lowest level of the economic and social scale has to work with his hands; he who belongs to the "better classes" gives proof of it by disdaining manual labour. This ethos of the Eastern economic mind is often noticed by Western visitors, and not very flatteringly styled as oriental laziness.[12]

The relationship between the poor and the rich may be organized in a variety of ways – including arrangements not entirely unfavourable for the peasant.[13] At the cost of some oversimplification one may distinguish three different types of characteristic peasant-landlord relationships: *patronage, partnership* and *exploitation*. The idea of patronage implies a mutual relationship between the wealthy and influential patron and the peasant. The patron protects his client and feels responsible for the survival of his client and his client's family; in return, the peasant pays a certain portion of his crop. Thus, the landlord shares part of the risk, since in years of a bad harvest he will get only a small payment or none at all or may even be put in the position of being like Job in the 29th chapter – a distributing "father to the needy". One passage in Deuteronomy suggests that poor people who own no land travel very far – even by sea – in order to find a wealthy patron who would "buy" their labour and give them food and shelter (Deut.

28:68). In a partnership arrangement the merchant provides materials, e.g. a weaving loom and wool, so that the peasant or his wife may produce for the urban bazaar and have some extra income. Or sharecropping contracts may stipulate a fifty-fifty distribution of the yield, thus leading to village prosperity in times of good harvest.

The third type is exploitation, based on the landowner's or creditor's interest in profit-making which excludes any personal loyalty to or reciprocity with the tenant or debtor. This estrangement is favoured by the landowner's urban residence ("absentee landlordism") as well as by the situation of the upper class which provides both for social prestige and political influence independent of any clientele support.

The consequences are reported by Lambton in her book on *Landlord and Peasant in Persia*:

> Between the landowner as a class, no matter what his origin, and the peasant there is a wide gulf. In no sense is there a spirit of co-operation or a feeling of being engaged in a mutual enterprise. The attitude is on the whole, though not without exceptions, one of mutual suspicion. The landowner regards the peasant virtually as a drudge, whose sole function is to provide him with his profits and who will, if treated with anything but severity, cheat him of his due. It is widely believed in landowning circles that anything above the barest consideration of the well-being of the peasant would be taken by the latter as a sign of weakness, and as a result he would not pay the dues of the landowner.[14]

The different arrangements – patronage, partnership, exploitation – alternately have had their impact on the economic history of the Near East. Urban entrepreneurship invites partnership; rural residence of the rich and democratic or quasi-democratic political constitution favour a patron-client relationship, because a patron may be dependent on entourage, co-operation and support. As soon as the market is able to provide luxury goods and gives rise to a corresponding urban life-style – which was the case in antiquity and has been true especially after the middle of the previous century – then exploitation may be a consequence.

In biblical Israel we can distinguish between two different systems of credit available to the small peasant. According to the first, the peasant goes to a kinsman to borrow some money or he sells him a plot of land, perhaps to get it back with the duty to pay some regular rent. Thus, the better-off kinsman takes over a patron's role as, e.g., does the urban resident Jeremiah, who buys a field of one of his village kinsmen.[15] The other credit system is based on the market and does not make use of any kinship connections. In this case the creditor may be extremely merciless and, as we know from Nathan's famous parable, may take the poor man's only sheep out of the fold.[16] Unfortunately, we cannot say under what circumstances the one or the other credit system was resorted to; both systems seem to operate at the same time. One may suggest that Jeremiah's kinsman uses the seventeen silver shekels he gets from the prophet to pay for his debts in the market and thus changes the credit system. Be this as it may – the two systems and their consequences are quite different for the debtor, as the generosity and amity usually shown towards a kinsman have no place in the market and are supplanted by pure calculation of profit.

Rent capitalism has left its imprint on the Near East and the results are still visible today: there is a marked contrast between the splendour of the cities and the misery of the countryside.[17] To be sure, you can see beggars in towns, but there are no urban proletarians as in classical Athens or Rome. The poor live in the country as fellaheen or hired labourers, but not in urban slums (which are a rather recent phenomenon in the Near East).[18] As the parasites, living off the countryside, the cities skim off a substantial portion of the proceeds of agricultural production leaving for the pauperized fellaheen hardly the means for their bare existence. We have a stagnating traditional culture and society at a very low ebb, in fact in a state of decadence not witnessed before. The philosopher, Oswald Spengler, took the "fellah people" of Egypt to illustrate what comes after the decline and final breakdown of a major civilization.[19] However, the decline does not affect everything: technology and the economic system become more and more nearly static and sterile, while in the urban culture the fine arts, literature, philosophy, religion and law – to name but a few disciplines – are fostered and often flourishing. The contrast between the primitive rural culture and the sophisticated urban civilization can hardly be exaggerated. It was only the advent of rent capitalism's younger brother, "productive capitalism", with its organization of labour in factories, national insurance and rural development which could provide the basis for technological progress and new (though not always better) social conditions.

Rent Capitalism and the Book of Amos

Now I will try to show how these social and economic conditions are reflected in the Book of Amos. The prophet accuses Israel or, more precisely, its upper classes, of exploitation and oppression of the peasant population. According to him, their behaviour deserves a punishment of the most severe kind. Amos threatens them with a political disaster mentioning mass deportation to a foreign country. Israel was situated on the periphery of the Assyrian empire and became more and more conscious of the growing influence and claims of the Assyrians. Already one hundred years before Amos, in 841 B.C., the Israelite king Jehu paid tribute to the Assyrian overlord. The monumental record of this incident, now on display in the British Museum and available as a postcard, shows King Jehu kissing the dust in front of his overlord Shalmaneser.[20]

In 1967, an Assyrian inscription was found that mentions an Israelite payment dating from 797,[21] and with this document we are almost in the generation of Amos whose prophetic activity is around 760. However, we are not going to deal with Israel's foreign and military policy, but with its domestic situation as it is sharply criticized by the prophet.

Quite often the rich are townspeople, who indulge in drinking and lead a life of shameless luxury.
For urban residence one can refer to Amos 6:1–8:

> Shame on you who live at ease in Zion,
> and you, untroubled on the hill of Samaria ...
> I loathe the arrogance of Jacob [i.e., Israel],
> I loathe his palaces [or, magnificent houses]:
> the city and all in it I will abandon to their fate.

The poetic text requires some explanation. The passage speaks of the capital of the northern Israelite kingdom, Samaria. It is situated on a mound justifying the expression "hill of Samaria". The parallel term "Zion" does not refer to Jerusalem as it does elsewhere, but is metaphorically applied to Samaria.[22] The prophet's "shame on you" (the "woe" of the older translations) is directed towards the rich who either live permanently in the capital or have an extra residence in town where they spend most of their time, far off from their landed property. (We know that Jeremiah was living in Jerusalem but had landed property at Anathoth.) Another text which mentions the city is Amos 4:1, where the prophet addresses the women; he says to them, "You cows of Bashan who live on the hill of Samaria, you who oppress the poor, and crush the destitute (etc.)". Comparing women to the well-fed cows of the Bashan region seems impolite as it violates our notion of female beauty, but in fact, even in the contemporary Near East, some well-to-do women do not care much for a slim body.

Open the book of Amos and you will find urban luxury and extravagance in almost every page: the rich have separate residences for winter and summer (3:15), built of fine ashlar stones (5:11); their furniture is decorated with beautiful carved work of ivory, now well known from archaeological finds (3:15; 6:4). Amos 6:4 – "Shame on you who loll on beds inlaid with ivory and sprawl over your couches" – does not attack wealth only, but also *la dolce vita*. On the later subject see also Amos 2:7: "Father and son resort to the same girl." According to Amos, the rich spend most of their time feasting; their luxuriant parties are in temples (2:8) or private houses (6:4ff.). As for the temple parties, the expression "in the house of their god" is of particular interest: the parties take place in the temple of the clan's patron deity who is not necessarily identical with Israel's national god, Yahweh. This does not imply any prophetic criticism of some unorthodox cult; to be sure, Amos speaks in the name of Yahweh, but he does not encourage Yahweh-alone worship, the promotion of which rests with a small minority, possibly led by Hosea. What is needed for feasting is almost always referred to more than once. Wine takes the first place: 2:8; 4:1; 6:6. The last-named passage refers to the big cups used for drinking – the "bowls" of the English translations imply some mild understatement. Amos 4:1 quotes the command, "Bring us drink", addressed to husbands, thus suggesting female dipsomania. In addition to wine we hear of "fatted calves" (5:22; 6:4), perfume (6:6), music and singing (5:23; 6:5). This refined banqueting, drinking and feasting culture is not confined to Samaria, of course; in the late eighth century it has its firm place in Isaiah's Jerusalem.[23] In this context Isaiah gives us a list of female jewellery and attire precious not only to the historian of culture; among its twenty-one items you can find familiar fancy articles such as ear-rings and necklaces but also lesser-known ones such as nose-rings and anklets. These women must have loved to load themselves with ornaments literally from head to foot! Some commentators have suggested that Isaiah, the townsman, was more familiar with the details of luxury than Amos, the villager.

As for the provenance of luxury goods no more than an informed guess is possible. The fine ivory carvings of this period found at Samaria by archaeologists may be local work but reveal Phoenician style, and it is self-evident that the expensive ivory was imported.[24] Most probably, the craze for precious ornaments never died out in Israelite towns and was often influenced by foreign fashion. Nobody wants to be inferior to other countries' upper classes, and capable dealers succeed in selling their stock. Palestine, and especially its northern part, is very fertile and gets enough rain; since time immemorial wheat and olive oil have been exported to Tyre in exchange for timber[25] and, possibly, all kinds of fashionable and beautiful smallware. One generation after Amos, when Israel finally loses the rest of its political independence, its crop goes to Assyria – now of course as a regular payment and hence without a corresponding economic return. Nothing but successive locust plagues prevent wealthy Samaria from paying its tribute – as a document of the Assyrian state archives reports.[26]

The upper class of the days of Amos and Isaiah shows all the features of Thorstein Veblen's "Theory of the Leisure Class", a book originally meant to criticize the American aristocracy of money by revealing its affluent life style and preference for meaningless activities (such as sports, hunting and academic study) and unproductive professions (such as merchant and diplomat). The members of the leisure class or – to use an expression of the German Middle Ages – "honourable idlers" (*ehrbare Müßiggänger*) do not produce anything, but rather consume according to the standards of conspicuous consumption, conspicuous waste and conspicuous leisure and pleasure. Consumption, extravagance and leisure are unlimited and constitute features of prestige or status symbols to be publicly displayed. The leisure class lives parasitically at the expense of the working class and does nothing but feast night and day. See Isa. 5:11–12:

Shame on you! You rise early in the morning

> to go in pursuit of liquor
> and draw out the evening inflamed with wine,
> at whose feasts there are harp and lute,
> tabor and pipe and wine.

And see Isa. 56:12:

> "Come", says each of them, "let me fetch wine,
> strong drink, and we will drain it down;
> let us make tomorrow like today,
> or greater far!"

And again Amos:

> Assemble on the hills of Samaria,
> look at the tumult seething among her people (3:9).

Landed property is often cultivated by small tenants liable to tax who are ruthlessly exploited by their landlords.

Amos reports more than once that the rich are taking advantage of their debtors or tenants,[27] their poor clientele. Amos 2:8 must be translated as follows:

> Men lie down beside every altar on blankets
> seized in pledge,
> and in the house of their [clan] god
> they drink wine got by way of exaction.

Fine blankets and wine – basic requirements for temple parties – are taken from debtors or tenants. Amos 4:1 – the oppressive women's categorical "bring us drink!" – seems to point to the same source of supply. Equally, Amos 5:11 refers to payments of crop. According to the New English Bible, the passage says: "Because you levy taxes on the poor and extort a tribute of grain from them ...", but a more accurate translation may be, "Because you make tenants out of the weak, and take tribute of corn from him."[28] The same passage explains what the landlords do with the extorted riches: they build beautiful "houses of hewn stone" and plant "pleasant vineyards" – possibly for letting them out on lease. Investing income to open up new sources of gain is known from the capable wife of Proverbs (Prov. 31:16) and belongs to the business of rich capital owners living on rents.

Peasants overburdened with debts have to sell themselves into bondage to work off their liabilities. The bondsmen become serfs liable to tax –

or they are even sold and thus become real and permanent slaves.

This can be demonstrated on the basis of Amos 2:6 and 8:6; however, both texts have to be analysed very carefully as the standard translations are misleading. But as I have presented the cultural background involved and all the arguments elsewhere,[29] let me just state the results.

In an imagined speech the wealthy upper-class people are made to say, "Let us buy the poor because of silver [i.e., debts of money), the needy because of a pair of sandals" (Amos 8:6). Two details require some explanation: How can you actually "buy" a debtor, and what is the matter with the sandals? They are the reason for buying the debtor. The symbolic action of giving a sandal is a feature of concluding an agreement or a transaction; this is understood from Ruth 4:7 which says, "It was the custom for a man to pull off his sandal and give it to the other party. This was the form of attestation in Israel." The sandal given to one's partner is the pledge for transferred property. Hence, the Hebrew word *na'alayim*, "a pair of sandals", acquired the meaning of "bond". Applied to our passage of Amos: the poor man is being "bought" because of a bond or obligation.

But what is the meaning of "to buy"? The context states quite clearly how the poor met the rich: as customers of the grain merchants. Viewed from outside, the poor buy the merchant's grain, but actually it is the merchant who buys his clients, that is to say: he makes them dependent on him, so that they become his permanent debtors and bondsmen. In fact, this was felt by Luther who translated, "wir wollen die Dürfigen unter uns bringen", i.e., "Let us subjugate the needy." The text suggests just this. The poor cannot pay for the grain bought for consumption or sowing, run into debt, pile up interest payments, and end up with that slave-like bondage which is so characteristic of rent capitalism.

Moreover, the relationship between creditor and debtor attains its full harshness only in the exploitation-variety of rent capitalism. As long as the rich feels a patron's responsibility, such harshness does not arise. To have to borrow because of poverty is always humiliating, but under the patronage system debtor and creditor stand within a network of mutual obligation and solidarity – the client being cared for by his patron, at least being prevented from starving. Once this network is broken, the creditor no longer acknowledges any responsibility for his debtor and uses him as a source of income. The debtor, always in a precarious situation, is now even more estranged and becomes a depersonalized object to be exploited. Since the law prohibiting the taking of interest belongs to the social legislation of the period of the exile, and thus to early Judaism,[30] it was incapable of protecting the debtor during the Israelite monarchy. Deut. 23:21 – a passage attesting the prohibition – reveals the actual relation between creditor and debtor: originally, interest is not taken from someone who happens to be a stranger, but rather the person from whom one extracts interest is considered a stranger. Later, the practices used to get around the condemnation not only of usury but of any kind of interest are legion.

In Amos 2:6 we can see how far the estrangement can go. The prophet reproaches his contemporaries for "selling the innocent because of silver [i.e., debts of money] and the poor because of a pair of sandals". In this case the poor are not bought but rather sold, cleared away by selling. They are not just reduced to being serfs or bondsmen but become slaves disjoined from their kinsmen who cannot buy them back any more.[31] What is the legal basis for such a sale? As a matter of fact, Israel's law as transmitted in the Bible does not provide any grounds for taking such action. On the other hand, exporting debtors to foreign countries is known from classical antiquity, namely from Rome and Greece. Its basis is easily understandable: to prevent the development of a poor and dependent class of proletarians in the community, debtors are disposed of by selling them abroad. Such deported persons are called "innocent" by our prophet, the Hebrew term *ṣaddiq* possibly implying a legal context. Granted this assumption we may infer a court order and consider the deportation as a legal measure. The prophet seems to reproach a legal yet unfair and unjust sentence, which bestows material advantages on the wealthy demandant and does away with the insolvent and perhaps insubordinate bondsmen. The court pronouncing such sentence must not be imagined as a centralized royal institution of superior authority, for the Israelite legal system has always been decentralized and local, with the adult male members of village or town forming the forum for the administration of justice. Hence, the poor were at the mercy of the landed proprietors themselves.

Along with rent and interest, the corn trade is another important source of income of the upper classes and strengthens their position in the economy.

Having repeatedly referred to one aspect of Amos 8:4–6 we are now in the position to understand this passage as a whole. It reads:

Listen to this, you who grind the destitute
and plunder the humble,
you who say, "When will the new moon be over
so that we may sell corn?
When will the sabbath [i.e., full moon] be past
so that we may open our wheat again,
giving short measure in the bushel
and taking overweight in the silver
tilting the scales fraudulently,
and selling the dust of the wheat;
that we may buy the poor because of silver
    [i.e., debts of money]
and the destitute because of a pair of sandals?"

Amos is secretly listening to a (fictitious) speech which reveals the corn dealers' brutality and fraud. New moon and full moon – the latter not to be understood as the weekly sabbath of the exile period – appear to be days where shops are closed and no transactions possible. Impatiently thinking of their usurious and fraudulent business the corn dealers can hardly await the end of the holidays. In years of hard harvest the peasants are likely to buy grain to survive. Likewise, day labourers depend on buying corn. Prov. 11:26 alludes to the practice of hoarding grain in seasons of scarcity in order to sell it at a high price:

He who withholds his grain is cursed by the people,
but he who sells his corn is blessed.

This proverb praises corn dealers who do not hold back their stock until starving customers are willing to pay any price demanded even for the worst quality – for they need food: for their family, themselves and perhaps for their cattle.

In saying all this I am well aware that I am going slightly beyond the information given in the biblical sources. But read in the light of anthropology, the scattered bits of economic and social information fit into a definite and clear picture known as rent capitalism. Everything finds, so to speak, its natural place.

NOTES

1   Karl Marx, *Capital*, ET David Fernbach, vol. 3 (Harmondsworth: Penguin, 1981) 731f.

2　The Hebrew term for "to conspire" (*qašar*), generally used for activities resulting in the murder of a king (1 Kgs 16:16; 2 Kgs 12:21), is central fo Amaziah's denunciation: Amos 7:10. For the politics of Amos and Hosea see: Bernhard Lang, *Monotheism and the Prophetic Minority* (Sheffield: Almond, 1983) 85f.; for the practice of remission of debts by royal decree see Jer. 34:8-22 (minus the secondary verses 13b–15a); N. P. Lemche, "The Manumission of Slaves", *VT* 26 (1976) 38–59.

3　Robert Redfield, *Peasant Society and Culture* (Chicago: Univ. of Chicago Press, 1956) 35–66; Eric R. Wolf, *Peasants* (Englewood Cliffs, N.J.: Prentice-Hall, 1966) 2ff., 48–57; G. Dalton, "Peasantries in Anthropology and History", *CA* 13 (1972) 385–415.

4　Gen. 2:24; Deut. 5:14 (to be understood of unmarried children); 23:30. The extended family called "the father's house" is a patrilineal lineage of three to four generations (Lev. 18:6–18; Josh. 7:17f.); it is no economic unit but may extend help to members in need.

5　Hans Bobek, "The Main Stages in Socio-economic Evolution from a Geographical Point of View", in *Readings in Cultural Geography*, ed. P. L. Wagner, M. W. Mikesell (Chicago: Univ. of Chicago Press, 1962) 218–47; Oswald Loretz, "Die prophetische Kritik des Rentenkapitalismus", *Ugarit-Forschungen* 7 (1975) 271–8.

6　Eugen Wirth, *Agrargeographie des Irak* (Berlin: de Gruyter, 1962) 20f.

7　Eugen Wirth, *Syrien* (Darmstadt: Wissenschaftliche Buchgesellschaft, 1971) 219. For "mechanisms of growing indebtedness" see E. Ehlers. *Iran* (Darmstadt: Wissenschaftliche Buchgesellschaft, 1980) 235f.

8　Papyrus Cowley 10 and 11: Pierre Grelot, *Documents araméens d'Egypte* (Paris: Editions du Cerf, 1972) 78–84. Further evidence is quoted by R. P. Maloney, "Usury and Restrictions on Interest-Taking in the Ancient Near East", *CBQ* 36 (1974) 1–20.

9　J. J. Janssen, "Die Struktur der pharaonischen Wirtschaft", *Göttinger Miszellen* 48 (1981) 59–77, on p. 70. For the "downwards mobility" of peasants see Neh. 5:1–13.

10　For classes *within* a village see Abdulla M. Lutfiyya, *Baytin. A Jordanian Village* (The Hague: Mouton, 1966) 32ff., 106f.

11　Debt bondage and slavery are, of course, not the same thing. In the Bible debt bondage is much more prominent, cf. Bernhard Lang, "Sklaven und Unfreie im Buch Amos", *VT* 31 (1981) 482–8. Finley, speaking of classical antiquity, insists that "slavery was a late and relatively infrequent form of involuntary labour, in world history generally and in ancient history in particular". He explains that "the common pattern until the Roman Empire seems to have been one of urban slavery and rural dependent, rather than slave, labour". Moses I. Finley, *Ancient Slavery and Modern Ideology* (New York: Viking, 1980) 77, 79.

12　Eugen Wirth, "Der heutige Irak als Beispiel orientalischen Wirtschaftsgeistes", in *Wirtschaftsgeographie*, ed. Eugen Wirth, 391–421 (Darmstadt: Wissenschaftliche Buchgesellschaft, 1969).

13　J. Scott, "Patronage or Exploitation?", in *Patrons and Clients in Mediterranean*

Societies, ed. Ernest Gellner, John Waterbury, 21–39 (London: Duckworth, 1977). That exploitation in terms of the rent capitalist system correlates with the political stability (Eugen Wirth, "Die Beziehungen der orientalischen Stadt zum umgebenden Land", in *Geographie heute – Einheit und Vielfalt,* 323–32 [Wiesbaden: Steiner, 1973], 328ff.) and the emergence of a domestic market bound to foreign exports and based on money as the medium of exchange, and a centralized bureaucracy (Iliya F. Harik, "The Impact of the Domestic Market on Rural-Urban Relations in the Middle East", in *Rural Politics and Social Change in the Middle East,* ed. Richard Antoun, I. Harik, 337–63 [Bloomington, Ind.: Indiana Univ. Press, 1972]) since the mid-nineteenth century may be true, but it seems that rent capitalism as such antedates the nineteenth century. Equally, situations lacking stability may lead the rent capitalist to exploit peasants as long as he is able to do so (Wolf, *Peasants,* 56). Usury, taking of high interest, and the peasants' dependence on urban credit facilities and landlords is, e.g., characteristic of the Near East in the eighteenth century as well, see Constantin-François de Volney, *Voyage en Syrie et en Egypte,* vol. 2 (Paris: Volland, 1787) 372–9; Albert H. Hourani, "The Fertile Crescent in the Eighteenth Century", *Studia Islamica* 8 (1957) 91–118.

14 A. K. S. Lambton, *Landlord and Peasant in Persia* (London: OUP, 1953) 263.

15 Jer. 32:6–15.

16 2 Sam. 12:1–4. Job 24:3 reflects similar conditions.

17 Wirth, "Die Beziehungen der orientalischen Stadt", 332.

18 Max Radin, *The Life of the People in Biblical Times* (Philadelphia: Jewish Publication Society, 1929) 113.

19 "That which follows a Culture we may call – from its best-known example – fellah-peoples." Oswald Spengler, *The Decline of the West,* vol. 2 (London: G. Allen & Unwin, 1928) 169.

20 The illustration is from *Bibel-Lexikon,* ed. Herbert Haag, 2nd edn (Einsiedeln: Benziger, 1968) 809.

21 Stephanie Page, "Joash and Samaria in a New Stela Excavated at Tell al Rimah, Iraq", *VT* 19 (1969) 483–4.

22 Georg Fohrer, "Sion", *TWNT* 7 (1963), 291–318; see p. 294.

23 Isa. 3:16—4:1; 5:11f.

24 From the Sudan: J. W. and G. M. Crowfoot, *Early Ivories from Samaria* (London: Palestine Exploration Fund, 1938) 54f.

25 1 Kgs 5:20–5; Ezra 3:7; Ezek. 27:17.

26 Robert H. Pfeiffer, *State Letters of Assyria* (New Haven: American Oriental Society, 1935) no. 97, read in the light of K. Deller in *Orientalia* 31 (1962) 234f.

27 This is, however, not without problems. Land tenure is well known from both the New Testament and post-biblical Jewish legal sources, but its existence cannot be demonstrated for the OT period. The first unquestionable attestation is a contract document found in Egypt dating from 515 B.C., see Grelot, *Documents araméens,* 71–5.

28 James A. Mays, *Amos.* OTL (London: SCM, 1969) 90.

29 Lang, "Sklaven und Unfreie".

30 In Deut. 23:20; Lev. 25:36; Ezek. 18:17 the exilic period asks for an exceptionally high measure of national solidarity. The older legislation in Exod. 22:24 seems to forbid exaggerated rates of interest rather than interest taking as such; the second part of the commandment forbidding to take any interest at all seems to be a secondary addition. Cf. Hendrik Bolkestein, *Wohltätigkeit und Armenpflege im vorchristlichen Altertum* (Groningen: Bouman's Boekhuis, 1967) 64: "In order to understand the social meaning of this prohibition [of interest taking] one has to keep in mind that the Israelites, before their dispersion throughout the ancient world, were not a merchant, but a peasant people. What we have here is a well-known piece of peasant morality. Credit is not given in order to allow for *production*, but to help someone, normally a peasant, out of an actual emergency. In other words: credit is given for *consumption*."

31 Franz Steiner, "Enslavement and the Early Hebrew Lineage System", *Man* 54 (1954) 73–5 = ch. 1 of this volume. In classical antiquity, too, slaves were denied the most elementary of social bonds, kinship: Finley, *Ancient Slavery*, 75f.

6

The Abominations of Leviticus[*]

MARY DOUGLAS

Defilement is never an isolated event. It cannot occur except in view of a systematic ordering of ideas. Hence any piecemeal interpretation of the pollution rules of another culture is bound to fail. For the only way in which pollution ideas make sense is in reference to a total structure of thought whose keystone, boundaries, margins and internal lines are held in relation by rituals of separation.

To illustrate this I take a hoary old puzzle from biblical scholarship, the abominations of Leviticus, and particularly the dietary rules. Why should the camel, the hare and the rock badger be unclean? Why should some locusts, but not all, be unclean? Why should the frog be clean and the mouse and the hippopotamus unclean? What have chameleons, moles and crocodiles got in common that they should be listed together (Lev. 11:27)?

To help follow the argument I first quote the relevant passages of Leviticus and Deuteronomy using the text of the Revised Standard Version.

Deuteronomy 14:3–18

[3]You shall not eat any abominable thing. [4]These are the animals you may eat:
the ox, the sheep, the goat, [5]the hart, the gazelle, the roebuck, the wild goat, the ibex, the antelope, and the mountain-sheep. [6]Every animal that parts the hoof and has the hoof cloven in two, and chews the cud, among the animals, you may eat. [7]Yet of those that chew the cud or have the hoof cloven you shall not eat

Leviticus 11:2–19

[2]These are the living things which you may eat among all the beasts that are on the earth.

[3]Whatever parts the hoof and is cloven-footed and chews the cud, among the animals, you may eat. [4]Nevertheless among those that chew the cud or part the hoof, you shall not eat these: The

---

[*]First published in *Purity and Danger* by Mary Douglas (1966) 41–57.

these: the camel,

the hare, and the rock badger, because they chew the cud but do not part the hoof, are unclean for you. [8]And the swine, because it parts the hoof but does not chew the cud, is unclean for you. Their flesh you shall not eat, and their carcasses you shall not touch.

[9]Of all that are in the waters you may eat these: whatever has fins and scales you may eat. [10]And whatever does not have fins and scales you shall not eat; it is unclean for you.

[11]You may eat all clean birds. [12]But these are the ones which you shall not eat: the eagle, the vulture, the osprey, [13]the buzzard, the kite, after their kinds, [14]every raven after its kind; [15]the ostrich, the nighthawk, the sea gull, the hawk, after their kinds; [16]the little owl and the great owl, the water hen [17]and the pelican, the carrion vulture and the cormorant, [18]the stork, the heron, after their kinds; the hoopoe and the bat.

camel, because it chews the cud but does not part the hoof, is unclean to you. [5]And the rock badger, because it chews the cud but does not part the hoof, is unclean to you. [6]And the hare, because it chews the cud but does not part the hoof, is unclean to you. [7]And the swine, because it parts the hoof and is cloven-footed but does not chew the cud, is unclean to you. [8]Of their flesh you shall not eat, and their carcasses you shall not touch; they are unclean to you.

[9]These you may eat, of all that are in the waters. Everything in the waters that has fins and scales, whether in the seas or in the rivers, you may eat. [10]But anything in the seas or the rivers that has not fins and scales, of the swarming creatures in the waters and of the living creatures that are in the waters, is an abomination to you. [11]They shall remain an abomination to you; of their flesh you shall not eat, and their carcasses you shall have in abomination. [12]Everything in the waters that has not fins and scales is an abomination to you.

[13]And these you shall have in abomination among the birds, they shall not be eaten, they are an abomination: the eagle, the vulture, the osprey, [14]the kite, the falcon according to its kind, [15]every raven according to its kind, [16]the ostrich, the nighthawk, the sea gull, the hawk according to its kind, [17]the owl, the cormorant, the ibis, [18]the water hen, the pelican, the carrion vulture, [19]the stork, the heron according to its kind, the hoopoe, and the bat.

Deuteronomy 14:19–20

[19]And all winged insects are unclean for you; they shall not be eaten. [20] All clean winged things you may eat.

Leviticus 11:20–42

[20]All winged insects that go upon all fours are an abomination to you. [21]Yet among the winged insects that go on all fours you may eat those which have legs above their feet, with which to leap on

101

Lev. 11:20–42 (cont.)

the earth. ²²Of them you may eat: the
locust according to its kind, the bald
locust according to its kind, the cricket
according to its kind, and the grasshopper
according to its kind. ²³But all other
winged insects which have four feet are
an abomination to you.

²⁴And by these you shall become unclean; whoever touches their carcass shall
be unclean until the evening, ²⁵and,
whoever carries any part of their carcass
shall wash his clothes and be unclean
until the evening. ²⁶Every animal which
parts the hoof but is not cloven-footed
or does not chew the cud is unclean to
you; every one who touches them shall
be unclean. ²⁷And all that go on their
paws, among the animals that go on all
fours, are unclean to you; whoever
touches their carcass shall be unclean
until the evening, ²⁸and he who carries
their carcass shall wash his clothes and
be unclean until the evening; they are
unclean to you.

²⁹And these are unclean to you among
the swarming things that swarm upon the
earth: the weasel, the mouse, the great
lizard according to its kind, ³⁰the gecko,
the land crocodile, the lizard, the sand
lizard, and the chameleon. ³¹These are
unclean to you among all that swarm;
whoever touches them when they are dead
shall be unclean until the evening. ³²And
anything upon which any of them falls
when they are dead shall be unclean,
whether it is an article of wood or a
garment or a skin or a sack, any vessel
that is used for any purpose; it must be
put into water, and it shall be unclean
until the evening; then it shall be clean.
³³And if any of them falls into any
earthen vessel, all that is in it shall be
unclean, and you shall break it. ³⁴Any
food in it which may be eaten, upon
which water may come, shall be unclean,
and all drink which may be drunk from
every such vessel shall be unclean. ³⁵And

Lev. 11:20–42 (cont.)

everything upon which any part of their carcass falls shall be unclean; whether oven or stove, it shall be broken in pieces; they are unclean, and shall be unclean to you. [36]Nevertheless a spring or a cistern holding water shall be clean; but whatever touches their carcass shall be unclean. [37]And if any part of their carcass falls upon any seed for sowing that is to be sown, it is clean; [38]but if water is put on the seed and any part of their carcass falls on it, it is unclean to you.

[39]And if any animal of which you may eat dies, he who touches its carcass shall be unclean until the evening, [40]and he who eats of its carcass shall wash his clothes and be unclean until the evening; he also who carries the carcass shall wash his clothes and be unclean until the evening. [41]Every swarming thing that swarms upon the earth is an abomination; it shall not be eaten. [42]Whatever goes on its belly, and whatever goes on all fours, or whatever has many feet, all the swarming things that swarm upon the earth, you shall not eat; for they are an abomination.

All the interpretations given so far fall into one of two groups: either the rules are meaningless, arbitrary because their intent is disciplinary and not doctrinal, or they are allegories of virtues and vices. Adopting the view that religious prescriptions are largely devoid of symbolism, Maimonides said:

The Law that sacrifices should be brought is evidently of great use ... but we cannot say why one offering should be a lamb whilst another is a ram, and why a fixed number of these should be brought. Those who trouble themselves to find a cause for any of these detailed rules are in my eyes devoid of sense.[1]

As a medieval doctor of medicine, Maimonides was also disposed to believe that the dietary rules had a sound physiological basis, but we have already dismissed the medical approach to symbolism. For a modern version of the view that the dietary rules are not symbolic, but ethical, disciplinary, see Epstein's English notes to the Babylonian Talmud and also his popular history of Judaism:

> Both sets of laws have one common aim ... Holiness. While the positive
> precepts have been ordained for the cultivation of virtue, and for the
> promotion of those finer qualities which distinguish the truly religious
> and ethical being, the negative precepts are defined to combat vice and
> suppress other evil tendencies and instincts which stand athwart man's
> striving towards holiness ... The negative religious laws are likewise
> assigned educational aims and purposes. Foremost among these is the
> prohibition of eating the flesh of certain animals classed as 'unclean'.
> This law has nothing totemic about it. It is expressly associated in
> Scripture with the ideal of holiness. Its real object is to train the Israelite
> in self-control as the indispensable first step for the attainment of
> holiness.[2]

According to Professor Stein's *The Dietary Laws in Rabbinic and
Patristic Literature*,[3] the ethical interpretation goes back to the time
of Alexander the Great and the Hellenic influence on Jewish culture.
The first-century A.D. Letter of Aristeas teaches that not only are
the Mosaic rules a valuable discipline which "prevents the Jews
from thoughtless action and injustice", but they also coincide with
what natural reason would dictate for achieving the good life. So
the Hellenic influence allows the medical and ethical interpretations
to run together. Philo held that Moses' principle of selection was
precisely to choose the most delicious meats:

> The lawgiver sternly forbade all animals of land, sea or air whose flesh
> is the finest and fattest, like that of pigs and scale-less fish, knowing that
> they set a trap for the most slavish of senses, the taste, and that they
> produce gluttony.

(and here we are led straight into the medical interpretation)

> an evil dangerous to both soul and body, for gluttony begets indigestion,
> which is the source of all illnesses and infirmities.[4]

In another stream of interpretation, following the tradition of
Robertson Smith and Frazer, the Anglo-Saxon OT scholars have
tended to say simply that the rules are arbitrary because they are
irrational. For example, Nathaniel Micklem says:

> Commentators used to give much space to a discussion of the question
> why such and such creatures, and such or such states and symptoms
> were unclean. Have we, for instance, primitive rules of hygiene? Or were
> certain creatures and states unclean because they represented or typified

certain sins? It may be taken as certain that neither hygiene, nor any kind of typology is the basis of uncleanness. These regulations are not by any means to be rationalised. Their origins may be diverse, and go back beyond history.[5]

Compare also S. R. Driver (1895):

> The principle, however, determining the line of demarcation between clean animals and unclean, is not stated: and what it is has been much debated. No single principle, embracing all the cases, seems yet to have been found, and not improbably more principles than one co-operated. Some animals may have been prohibited on account of their repulsive appearance or uncleanly habits, others upon sanitary grounds; in other cases, again, the motive of the prohibition may very probably have been a religious one, particularly animals may have been supposed, like the serpent in Arabia, to be animated by superhuman or demoniac beings, or they may have had a sacramental significance in the heathen rites of other nations; and the prohibition may have been intended as a protest against these beliefs.[6]

P. P. Saydon takes the same line in the *Catholic Commentary on Holy Scripture*,[7] acknowledging his debt to Driver and to Robertson Smith. It would seem that when Robertson Smith applied the ideas of primitive, irrational and unexplainable to some parts of Hebrew religion they remained thus labelled and unexamined to this day.

Needless to say such interpretations are not interpretations at all, since they deny any significance to the rules. They express bafflement in a learned way. Micklem says it more frankly when he writes of Leviticus:

> Chapters 11 to 15 are perhaps the least attractive in the whole Bible. To the modern reader there is much in them that is meaningless or repulsive ... They are concerned with ritual "uncleanness" in respect of animals (11), of childbirth (12), skin diseases and tainted garments (13), of the rites for the purgation of skin diseases (14:1–32), of "leprosy" in houses (14:33–57), and finally of various issues or secretions of the human body (15). Of what interest can such subjects be except to the anthropologist? What can all this have to do with religion?[8]

Pfeiffer's general position is to be critical of the priestly and legal elements in the life of Israel. So he too lends his authority to the view that the rules in the Priestly Code are largely arbitrary:

> Only priests who were lawyers could have conceived of religion as a theocracy regulated by a divine law fixing exactly, and therefore

arbitrarily, the sacred obligations of the people to their God. They thus sanctified the external, obliterated from religion both the ethical ideals of Amos and the tender emotions of Hosea, and reduced the Universal Creator to the stature of an inflexible despot ... From immemorial custom P derived the two fundamental notions which characterise its legislation: physical holiness and arbitrary enactment – archaic conceptions which the reforming prophets had discarded in favour of spiritual holiness and moral law.[9]

It may be true that lawyers tend to think in precise and codified forms. But is it plausible to argue that they tend to codify sheer nonsense – arbitrary enactments? Pfeiffer tries to have it both ways, insisting on the legalistic rigidity of the priestly authors and pointing to the lack of order in the setting out of the chapter to justify his view that the rules are arbitrary. Arbitrariness is a decidedly unexpected quality to find in Leviticus, as H. J. Richards has pointed out to me. For source criticism attributes Leviticus to the Priestly source, the dominant concern of whose authors was for order. So the weight of source criticism supports us in looking for another interpretation.

As for the idea that the rules are allegories of virtues and vices, Stein derives this vigorous tradition from the same early Alexandrian influence on Jewish thought.

Quoting the Letter of Aristeas, he says that the high priest, Eleazar:

admits that most people find the biblical food restrictions not understand-able. If God is the Creator of everything, why should His law be so severe as to exclude some animals even from touch [128f.]? His first answer still links the dietary restrictions with the danger of idolatry ... The second answer attempts to refute specific charges by means of allegorical exegesis. Each law about forbidden foods has its deep reason. Moses did not enumerate the mouse or the weasel out of a special consideration for them [143f.]. On the contrary, mice are particularly obnoxious because of their destructiveness, and weasels, the very symbol of malicious tale-bearing, conceive through the ear and give birth through the mouth [164f.]. Rather have these holy laws been given for the sake of justice to awaken in us devout thoughts and to form our character [161–8]. The birds, for instance, the Jews are allowed to eat are all tame and clean, as they live by corn only. Not so the wild and carnivorous birds who fall upon lambs and goats, and even human beings. Moses, by calling the latter unclean, admonished the faithful not to do violence to the weak and not to trust their own power [145–8]. Cloven-hoofed animals which part their hooves symbolise that all our actions must betray proper ethical distinction and be directed towards righteousness. ... Chewing the cud, on the other hand stands for memory.[10]

Professor Stein goes on to quote Philo's use of allegory to interpret the dietary rules:

> Fish with fins and scales, admitted by the law, symbolise endurance and self-control, whilst the forbidden ones are swept away by the current, unable to resist the force of the stream. Reptiles, wriggling along by trailing their belly, signify persons who devote themselves to their ever greedy desires and passions. Creeping things, however, which have legs above their feet, so that they can leap, are clean because they symbolise the success of moral efforts.[11]

Christian teaching has readily followed the allegorizing tradition. The first-century Epistle of Barnabas, written to convince the Jews that their Law had found its fulfilment, took the clean and unclean animals to refer to various types of men, leprosy to mean sin, etc. A more recent example of this tradition is in Bishop Challoner's notes on the Westminster Bible at the beginning of this century:

> Hoof divided and cheweth the cud. The dividing of the hoof and chewing of the cud signify discretion between good and evil, and meditating on the law of God; and where either of these is wanting, man is unclean. In like manner fishes were reputed unclean that had not fins and scales: that is souls that did not raise themselves up by prayer and cover themselves with the scale of virtue. (Footnote verse 3)

These are not so much interpretations as pious commentaries. They fail as interpretations because they are neither consistent nor comprehensive. A different explanation has to be developed for each animal and there is no end to the number of possible explanations.

Another traditional approach, also dating back to the Letter of Aristeas, is the view that what is forbidden to the Israelites is forbidden solely to protect them from foreign influence. For instance, Maimonides held that they were forbidden to seethe the kid in the milk of its dam because this was a cultic act in the religion of the Canaanites. This argument cannot be comprehensive, for it is not held that the Israelites consistently rejected all the elements of foreign religions and invented something entirely original for themselves. Maimonides accepted the view that some of the more mysterious commands of the Law had as their object to make

Mary Douglas

a sharp break with heathen practices. Thus the Israelites were forbidden to wear garments woven of linen and wool, to plant different trees together, to have sexual intercourse with animals, to cook meat with milk, simply because these acts figured in the rites of their heathen neighbours. So far, so good: the laws were enacted as barriers to the spread of heathen styles of ritual. But in that case why were some heathen practices allowed? And not only allowed – if sacrifice be taken as a practice common to heathens and Israelites – but given an absolutely central place in the religion. Maimonides' answer, at any rate in *The Guide for the Perplexed*, was to justify sacrifice as a transitional stage, regrettably heathen, but necessarily allowed because it would be impractical to wean the Israelites abruptly from their heathen past. This is an extraordinary statement to come from the pen of a rabbinical scholar, and indeed in his serious rabbinical writings Maimonides did not attempt to maintain the argument: on the contrary, he there counted sacrifice as the most important act of the Jewish religion.

At least Maimonides saw the inconsistency and was led by it into contradiction. But later scholars seem content to use the foreign influence argument one way or the other, according to the mood of the moment. Professor Hooke and his colleagues have clearly established that the Israelites took over some Canaanite styles of worship, and the Canaanites obviously had much in common with Mesopotamian culture.[12] But it is no explanation to represent Israel as a sponge at one moment and as a repellent the next, without explaining why it soaked up this foreign element but repelled that one. What is the value of saying that seething kids in milk and copulating with cows are forbidden in Leviticus because they are the fertility rites of foreign neighbours,[13] since Israelites took over other foreign rites? We are still perplexed to know when the sponge is the right or the wrong metaphor. The same argument is equally puzzling in Eichrodt.[14] Of course no culture is created out of nothing. The Israelites absorbed freely from their neighbours, but not quite freely. Some elements of foreign culture were incompatible with the principles of patterning on which they were constructing their universe; others were compatible. For instance, Zaehner suggests that the Jewish abomination of creeping things may have been taken over from Zoroastrianism.[15] Whatever the historical evidence for this adoption of a foreign element into Judaism, we shall see that there was in the patterning of their culture a pre-formed compatibility between this particular abomination and the general principles on which their universe was constructed.

108

Any interpretations will fail which take the Do-nots of the OT in piecemeal fashion. The only sound approach is to forget hygiene, aesthetics, morals and instinctive revulsion, even to forget the Canaanites and the Zoroastrian magi, and start with the texts. Since each of the injunctions is prefaced by the command to be holy, so they must be explained by that command. There must be contrariness between holiness and abomination which will make overall sense of all the particular restrictions.

Holiness is the attribute of Godhead. Its root means "set apart". What else does it mean? We should start any cosmological enquiry by seeking the principles of power and danger. In the OT we find blessing as the source of all good things, and the withdrawal of blessing as the source of all dangers. The blessing of God makes the land possible for men to live in.

God's work through the blessing is essentially to create order, through which men's affairs prosper. Fertility of women, livestock and fields is promised as a result of the blessing and this is to be obtained by keeping covenant with God and observing all his precepts and ceremonies (Deut. 28:1–14). Where the blessing is withdrawn and the power of the curse unleashed, there is barrenness, pestilence, confusion. For Moses said:

> But if you will not obey the voice of the Lord your God or be careful to do all his commandments and his statutes which I command you to this day, then all these curses shall come upon you and overtake you. Cursed shall you be in the city, and cursed shall you be in the field. Cursed shall be your basket and your kneading trough. Cursed shall be the fruit of your body, and the fruit of your ground, the increase of your cattle, and the young of your flock. Cursed shall you be when you come in and cursed shall you be when you go out. The Lord will send upon you curses, confusion, and frustration in all that you undertake to do, until you are destroyed and perish quickly on account of the evil of your doings, because you have forsaken me ... The Lord will smite you with consumption, and with fever, inflammation, and fiery heat, and with drought, and with blasting and with mildew; they shall pursue you till you perish. And the heavens over your head shall be brass and the earth under you shall be iron. The Lord will make the rain of your land powder and dust; from heaven it shall come down upon you until you are destroyed. (Deut. 28:15–24)

From this it is clear that the positive and negative precepts are held to be efficacious and not merely expressive: observing them draws down prosperity, infringing them brings danger. We are thus entitled to treat them in the same way as we treat primitive ritual avoidances whose breach unleashes danger to men. The precepts and ceremonies alike are focused on the idea of the holiness of God which men must create in their own lives. So this is a universe in which men prosper by conforming to holiness and perish when they deviate from it. If there were no other clues we should be able to find out the Hebrew idea of the holy by examining the precepts by which men conform to it. It is evidently not goodness in the sense of an all-embracing humane kindness. Justice and moral goodness may well illustrate holiness and form part of it, but holiness embraces other ideas as well.

Granted that its root means separateness, the next idea that emerges is of the Holy as wholeness and completeness. Much of Leviticus is taken up with stating the physical perfection that is required of things presented in the Temple and of persons approaching it. The animals offered in sacrifice must be without blemish, women must be purified before childbirth, lepers should be separated and ritually cleansed before being allowed to approach it once they are cured. All bodily discharges are defiling and disqualify from approach to the Temple. Priests may only come into contact with death when their own close kin die. But the high priest must never have contact with death.

> Lev. 21:17 Say to Aaron, None of your descendants throughout their generations who had a blemish may approach to offer the bread of his God. 18 For no one who has a blemish shall draw near, a man blind or lame, or one who has a mutilated face or a limb too long 19 or a man who has an injured foot or an injured hand, 20 or a hunch-back, or a dwarf, or a man with a defect in his sight or an itching disease or scabs, or crushed testicles; 21 no man of the descendants of Aaron the priest who has a blemish shall come near to offer the Lord's offerings by fire.

In other words, he must be perfect as a man, if he is to be a priest.

This much reiterated idea of physical completeness is also worked out in the social sphere and particularly in the warriors' camp. The culture of the Israelites was brought to the pitch of greatest intensity when they prayed and when they fought. The army could not win without the blessing, and to keep the blessing in the camp they had to be specially holy. So the camp was to be preserved from defilement like the Temple. Here again all bodily discharges disqualified a man from entering the camp as they would disqualify

110

a worshipper from approaching the altar. A warrior who had had an issue of the body in the night should keep outside the camp all day and only return after sunset, having washed. Natural functions producing bodily waste were to be performed outside the camp (Deut. 23:10–15). In short the idea of holiness was given an external, physical expression in the wholeness of the body seen as a perfect container.

Wholeness is also extended to signify completeness in a social context. An important enterprise, once begun, must not be left incomplete. This way of lacking wholeness also disqualifies a man from fighting. Before a battle the captains shall proclaim:

> Deut. 20:5 What man is there that has built a new house and has not dedicated it? Let him go back to his house, lest he die in the battle and another man dedicate it. 6 What man is there that has planted a vineyard and has not enjoyed its fruit? Let him go back to his house, lest he die in the battle and another man enjoy its fruit. 7 And what man is there that hath betrothed a wife and has not taken her? Let him go back to his house, lest he die in the battle and another man take her.

Admittedly there is no suggestion that this rule implies defilement. It is not said that a man with a half-finished project on his hands is defiled in the same way that a leper is defiled. The next verse in fact goes on to say that fearful and faint-hearted men should go home lest they spread their fears. But there is a strong suggestion in other passages that a man should not put his hand to the plough and then turn back. Pedersen goes so far as to say that:

> in all these cases a man has started a new important undertaking without having finished it yet . . . a new totality has come into existence. To make a breach in this prematurely, i.e. before it has attained maturity or has been finished, involves a serious risk of sin.[16]

If we follow Pedersen, then blessing and success in war required a man to be whole in body, wholehearted and trailing no uncompleted schemes. There is an echo of this actual passage in the NT parable of the man who gave a great feast and whose invited guests incurred his anger by making excuses.[17] One of the guests had bought a new farm, one had bought ten oxen and had not yet tried them, and one had married a wife. If according to the old Law each could have validly justified his refusal by reference to Deuteronomy 20 the parable supports Pedersen's view that interruption of new projects was held to be bad in civil as well as military contexts.

Other precepts develop the idea of wholeness in another direction.

111

The metaphors of the physical body and of the new undertaking relate to the perfection and completeness of the individual and his work. Other precepts extend holiness to species and categories. Hybrids and other confusions are abominated.

> Lev. 18:23 And you shall not lie with any beast and defile yourself with it, neither shall any woman give herself to a beast to lie with it: it is perversion.

The word "perversion" is a significant mistranslation of the rare Hebrew word *tebhel*, which has as its meaning mixing or confusion. The same theme is taken up in Lev. 19:19:

> You shall keep my statutes. You shall not let your cattle breed with a different kind: you shall not sow your field with two kinds of seed; nor shall there come upon you a garment of cloth made of two kinds of stuff.

All these injunctions are prefaced by the general command:

> Be holy, for I am holy.

We can conclude that holiness is exemplified by completeness. Holiness requires that individuals shall conform to the class to which they belong. And holiness requires that different classes of things shall not be confused.

Another set of precepts refines on this last point. Holiness means keeping distinct the categories of creation. It therefore involves correct definition, discrimination and order. Under this head all the rules of sexual morality exemplify the holy. Incest and adultery (Lev. 18:6–20) are against holiness, in the simple sense of right order. Morality does not conflict with holiness, but holiness is more a matter of separating that which should be separated than of protecting the rights of husbands and brothers.

Then follows in chapter 19 another list of actions which are contrary to holiness. Developing the idea of holiness as order, not confusion, this list upholds rectitude and straight-dealing as holy, and contradiction and double-dealing as against holiness. Theft, lying, false witness, cheating in weights and measures, all kinds of dissembling such as speaking ill of the deaf (and presumably smiling to their face), hating your brother in your heart (while presumably speaking kindly to him), these are clearly contradictions between what seems and what is. This chapter also says much about generosity and love, but these are positive commands, while I am concerned with negative rules.

We have now laid a good basis for approaching the laws about clean and unclean meats. To be holy is to be whole, to be one; holiness is unity, integrity, perfection of the individual and of the kind. The dietary rules merely develop the metaphor of holiness on the same lines.

First we should start with livestock, the herds of cattle, camels, sheep and goats which were the livelihood of the Israelites. These animals were clean inasmuch as contact with them did not require purification before approaching the Temple. Livestock, like the inhabited land, received the blessing of God. Both land and livestock were fertile by the blessing, both were drawn into the divine order. The farmer's duty was to preserve the blessing. For one thing, he had to preserve the order of creation. So no hybrids, as we have seen, either in the fields or in the herds or in the clothes made from wool or flax. To some extent men covenanted with their land and cattle in the same way that God covenanted with them. Men respected the first-born of their cattle, obliged them to keep the sabbath. Cattle were literally domesticated as slaves. They had to be brought into the social order in order to enjoy the blessing. The difference between cattle and the wild beasts is that the wild beasts have no covenant to protect them. It is possible that the Israelites were like other pastoralists who do not relish wild game. The Nuer of the south Sudan, for instance, apply a sanction of disapproval of a man who lives by hunting. To be driven to eating wild meat is the sign of a poor herdsman. So it would be probably wrong to think of the Israelites as longing for forbidden meats and finding the restrictions irksome. Driver is surely right in taking the rules as an *a posteriori* generalization of their habits. Cloven-hoofed, cud-chewing ungulates are the model of the proper kind of food for a pastoralist. If they must eat wild game, they can eat wild game that shares these distinctive characters and is therefore of the same general species. This is a kind of casuistry which permits scope for hunting antelope and wild goats and wild sheep. Everything would be quite straightforward were it not that the legal mind has seen fit to give ruling on some borderline cases. Some animals seem to be ruminant, such as the hare and the hyrax (or rock badger), whose constant grinding of their teeth was held to be cud-chewing. But they are definitely not cloven-hoofed and so are excluded by name. Similarly for animals which are cloven-hoofed but are not ruminant, the pig and the camel. Note that this failure to conform to the two necessary criteria for defining cattle is the only reason given in the OT for avoiding the pig; nothing whatever is said about its dirty scavenging habits. As the pig does not yield milk, hide nor wool, there is no other reason for keeping it except for its flesh. And if the Israelites did not keep pig they would not be familiar with its habits. I suggest that originally the sole reason for its being counted as unclean is its failure as a wild boar to get into the antelope class, and that in this it is on the same footing as the camel and the hyrax, exactly as is stated in the book.

After these borderline cases have been dismissed, the law goes on to deal with creatures according to how they live in the three elements, the water, the air and the earth. The principles here applied are rather different from those covering the camel, the pig, the hare and the hyrax. For the latter are excepted from clean food in having one but not both of the defining characters of livestock. Birds I can say nothing about, because as I have said, they are named and not described and the translation of the names is open to doubt. But in general the underlying principle of cleanness in animals is that they shall conform fully to their class. Those species are unclean which are imperfect members of their class, or whose class itself confounds the general scheme of the world.

To grasp this scheme we need to go back to Genesis and the creation. Here a threefold classification unfolds, divided between the earth, the waters and the firmament. Leviticus takes up this scheme and allots to each element its proper kind of animal life. In the firmament two-legged fowls fly with wings. In the water scaly fish swim with fins. On the earth four-legged animals hop, jump or walk. Any class of creatures which is not equipped for the right kind of locomotion in its element is contrary to holiness. Contact with it disqualifies a person from approaching the Temple. Thus anything in the water which has not fins and scales is unclean (11:10–12). Nothing is said about predatory habits or of scavenging. The only sure test for cleanness in a fish is its scales and its propulsion by means of fins.

Four-footed creatures which fly (11:20–6) are unclean. Any creature which has two legs and two hands and which goes on all fours like a quadruped is unclean (11:27). Then follows (v. 29) a much disputed list. On some translations, it would appear to consist precisely of creatures endowed with hands instead of front feet, which perversely use their hands for walking: the weasel, the mouse, the crocodile, the shrew, various kinds of lizards, the chameleon and mole, whose forefeet are uncannily hand-like. This feature of this list is lost in the new Revised Standard Version which uses the word "paws" instead of hands.

The last kind of unclean animal is that which creeps, crawls or swarms upon the earth. This form of movement is explicitly contrary to holiness (Lev. 11:41–4). Driver[18] uses "swarming" to translate the Hebrew *šeres*, which is applied to both those which teem in the waters and those which swarm on the ground. Whether we call it teeming, trailing, creeping, crawling or swarming, it is an indeterminate form of movement. Since the main animal categories are defined by their typical movement, "swarming" which is not a mode of propulsion proper to any particular element, cuts across the basic classification. Swarming things are neither fish, flesh nor fowl. Eels and worms inhabit water, though not as fish; reptiles go on dry land, though not as quadrupeds; some insects fly, though not as birds. There is no order in them. Recall what the prophecy of Habakkuk says about this form of life:

> For thou makest men like the fish of the sea, like crawling things that have no ruler. (Hab. 1:14)

The prototype and model of the swarming things is the worm. As fish belong in the sea so worms belong in the realm of the grave, with death and chaos.

The case of the locusts is interesting and consistent. The test of whether it is a clean and therefore edible kind is how it moves on the earth. If it crawls it is unclean. If it hops it is clean (11:21). In the Mishnah it is noted that a frog is not listed with creeping things and conveys no uncleanness.[19]

I suggest that the frog's hop accounts for it not being listed. If penguins lived in the Near East I would expect them to be ruled unclean as wingless birds. If the list of unclean birds could be translated from this point of view, it might well turn out that they are anomalous because they swim and dive as well as they fly, or in some other way they are not fully birdlike.

Surely now it would be difficult to maintain that "Be ye Holy" means no more than "Be ye separate". Moses wanted the children of Israel to keep the commands of God constantly before their minds:

> Deut. 11:18 You shall therefore lay up these words of mine in your heart and in your soul; and you shall bind them as a sign upon your head, and they shall be as frontlets between your eyes.
>
> 19 And you shall teach them to your children, talking of them when you are sitting in your house, and when you are walking by the way, and when you lie down and when you rise.

20 And you shall write them upon the doorposts of your house and upon your gates.

If the proposed interpretation of the forbidden animals is correct, the dietary laws would have been like signs which at every turn inspired meditation on the oneness, purity and completeness of God. By rules of avoidance holiness was given a physical expression in every encounter with the animal kingdom and at every meal. Observance of the dietary rules would thus have been a meaningful part of the great liturgical act of recognition and worship which culminated in the sacrifice in the Temple.

NOTES

1 Moses Maimonides, *The Guide for the Perplexed*, ET M. Friedländer (New York: Dover Publications, 1956) 311.

2 Isidore Epstein, *Judaism. A Historical Presentation* (Harmondsworth: Penguin, 1959) 24–5.

3 S. Stein, "The Dietary Laws in Rabbinic and Patristic Literature", *Texte und Untersuchungen zur Geschichte der altchristlichen Literatur* 64 (1957) 141–54.

4 Philo, *De specialibus legibus* 4:97ff.; quoted in Stein, "The Dietary Laws", 147.

5 *The Interpreter's Bible*, vol. 2 (New York: Abingdon, 1953) 54.

6 Samuel R. Driver, *Deuteronomy*. ICC (New York: Scribner, 1902) 164.

7 *A Catholic Commentary on Holy Scripture* (New York: Nelson, 1953).

8 *The Interpreter's Bible*, 52.

9 Robert H. Pfeiffer, *The Books of the Old Testament* (New York: Harper, 1957) 91.

10 Stein, "The Dietary Laws", 145f.

11 Stein, "The Dietary Laws", 147f.

12 *Myth and Ritual*, ed. S. H. Hooke (London: OUP, 1933).

13 Hooke, in *Myth and Ritual*, 71.

14 Walther Eichrodt, *Theology of the Old Testament*, vol. 1, ET J. A. Baker. OTL (London: SCM, 1961) 230f.

15 R. C. Zaehner, *The Dawn and Twilight of Zoroastrianism* (London: Weidenfeld & Nicholson, 1961) 162.

16 Johs. Pedersen, *Israel: its Life and Culture*, vol. 3–4 (London: OUP, 1940) 10.

17 Luke 14:16–24; Matt. 22. Cf. *Peake's Commentary on the Bible*, ed. Matthew Black, H. H. Rowley (Edinburgh: Nelson, 1962) 836.

18 Driver, *Deuteronomy*, 163.

19 Herbert Danby, *The Mishnah* (London: OUP, 1933) 722 with note 9.

7

One More Time:
*Leviticus Revisited**

MICHAEL P. CARROLL

Nothing is more likely to attract support for a new theory than showing that that theory can shed new light upon an old problem. This undoubtedly explains why the most well-known section of Mary Douglas' *Purity and Danger* (1966) is her section on the dietary prohibitions of Leviticus.[1] Her argument is appealing not only because she demonstrates that there is a consistent rationale which underlies these prohibitions, but also because the rationale that she discovers is quite unrelated to those explanations – vaguely based upon considerations of hygiene and allegory – typically offered. But despite the continuing visibility of the Douglas analysis, no one to my knowledge has critically examined her argument in detail. Such is the goal of this article.

The first half of the article will demonstrate that there is little textual support for many of the interpretations that Douglas must make in support of her argument, while the second half will present an alternative explanation of the dietary prohibitions. This alternative explanation will involve an application of Douglas' general theory that is quite different from the application of that theory that she herself develops.

Uncleanness and Anomaly

In *Purity and Danger*, Douglas argued: (1) that the unclean animals of Leviticus were anomalous with respect to the classification scheme established in the opening chapter of Genesis, (2) that they therefore threaten the integrity of that scheme, and (3) that for this reason they were ritually tabooed. In a more recent work[2] she recognizes

* First published in *AES* 19 (1978) 339–46.

that anomalous animals can be either tabooed or favourably evaluated depending upon the social structure of the society in question. In a society like ancient Israel, that favours endogamy within social groups, she expects that such animals will be tabooed; in other societies, that favour exchanges between social groups, she expects that such animals will be more favourably received. But she still retains her central premise, which is that the unclean animals are anomalous – and it is this premise that I wish to challenge.

Douglas argues that Genesis establishes a threefold classification of animals – "land animals", "water animals", and "flying animals" – and that anomalous animals are those that do not exhibit the mode of locomotion peculiar to one of these three classes. Yet if we review what is actually said in Genesis and count as an "important" animal category one that is mentioned at least twice then we arrive at the following list:

1 "fish" (Gen. 1: 26, 28)
2 "birds" (Gen. 1: 20, 21, 22, 26, 28)
3 "cattle" (Gen. 1: 24, 25, 26)
4 "beasts of the earth" (Gen. 1: 24, 25, 30)
5 "creeping things" (Gen. 1: 24, 25, 26, 30).

To be sure, it is possible to collapse the last three categories into a single category ("land animals"), but this would reflect the analytic preferences of the modern reader, and *not* the logic of Genesis, which is at pains to list separately these three categories, as in the following passage:

> Gen. 1:25: And God made the beasts of the earth according to their kinds and the cattle according to their kinds, and everything that creeps upon the ground according to its kind.

The next question is obvious: is it true, as would be suggested by Douglas' general theory, that those animals defined as unclean are also those animals anomalous with respect to this fivefold classification scheme?

Leviticus states that all land animals that do not chew the cud and part the hoof are unclean. Yet many of the land animals defined as unclean by this rule (including those mentioned in Leviticus, namely, the hare and the rock badger) would easily fit into the "beasts of the earth" category and thus are *not* anomalous.

Her theory, however, works quite well in connection with water creatures. Although Douglas does not mention it, there is some philological evidence[3] to suggest that the Hebrew term translated

118

as "fish" in Genesis refers to creatures that move about by the vibratory action of their fins and tail. Hence those water creatures that do not move about in this way are anomalous. Thus the fact that Leviticus defines as unclean those water creatures that lack "fins and scales" (Lev. 11:9–12) is perfectly consistent with the Douglas theory.

There is, however, much difficulty in Douglas' treatment of flying creatures. To be sure, in the Revised Standard Version of the OT, Genesis records "birds" as being created on the fifth day, and "birds" (as seems obvious to us all) are two-legged creatures. Hence Douglas' argument that "flying insects" (four-legged flying creatures) are defined as unclean in Lev. 11:20 because they are anomalous with respect to the "bird" category seems perfectly reasonable. Unfortunately, although "birds" and "flying insects" may seem to the modern reader to be quite separate categories, this is not really the case here. The Hebrew term that the Revised Standard Version translates as "birds" in Genesis (and again in Lev. 11:13) is really a generic term for a variety of flying creatures, including birds, bats, *and* flying insects.[4] The sense of all this is better conveyed in older translations which talk simply of the creation of "fowls" on the fifth day (in Genesis) and the prohibition (in Lev. 11:20) of those particular "fowls that creep, going upon all fours". In other words, two-legged fowls (birds) and four-legged fowls (flying insects) are just subcategories of the general "fowl" category established in Genesis. But because flying insects are not anomalous with respect to the classification scheme established in Genesis, Douglas' theory cannot really explain why they are defined as unclean.

Douglas goes on to argue that since most land animals are four-legged, "any creature which has two legs and two hands and which goes on all fours like a quadruped is unclean".[5] For her, this explains the prohibition against "swarming things" in Lev. 11:29. While indeed some of the animals specifically mentioned in this section of Leviticus (like the shrew and the mouse) would seem to have hand-like front appendages, others (like the crocodile and the weasel) do not.

More importantly, one of the textual interpretations Douglas makes in support of her argument here is quite unjustified. Lev. 11:27 specifically defines as unclean those four-legged land animals that "go down upon their paws". Douglas suggests that "hands" would be a more appropriate translation than "paws" in this passage.[6] In fact, she is only partly correct. The Hebrew term in question really refers to the *palm* of a hand or the *sole* of a foot.[7]

119

This has led most commentators to infer that what is being referred to here are animals that have *pads* on their feet, e.g. wolves, lions, bears, etc.[8] Unless one is prepared to argue that animals with pads on their feet have front appendages that are more "hand-like" than those of other quadrupeds (a premise that I personally would find difficult to accept), then the prohibition of "animals that go down upon their paws" provides no support for the Douglas argument.

Douglas' argument about "swarming things" is weak on other grounds as well. Remember that one of the three major categories of land animals established in Genesis was the "creeping things" category. This is usually taken to refer to the land-based reptiles such as lizards and snakes.[9] The "swarming things" category is broader, including not only land-based reptiles, but also insects, small quadrupeds and generally any animal that moves close to the ground. But the important point is that the "swarming things" category subsumes the "creeping things" category. In fact, of the eight "swarming things" specially listed in the Revised Standard Version of Leviticus (these being the weasel, the mouse, the great lizard, the gecko, the land crocodile, the lizard, the sand lizard, and t·e chameleon), the last six are land-based reptiles and would thus fall into the "creeping things" category as well. In other words, a majority of the "swarming things" specifically defined as unclean are not anomalous with respect to the classification scheme established in Genesis.

In response to all the criticism raised to this point, it is of course possible to read Douglas as saying that the animal classification scheme established in Genesis is irrelevant, and that it is Leviticus itself that associates each animal category with the "appropriate" sort of animal. But such an interpretation would make her argument tautological. Why are flying insects unclean? Because flying insects have four legs and flying creatures should appropriately have only two legs. Why should flying creatures appropriately have only two legs? Because all other types of flying creatures are defined as unclean in Leviticus!

An Alternative Explanation

The contribution of the preceding section has been for the most part negative, in that the primary goal was to bring out the weaknesses of the Douglas argument. It seems incumbent upon me to suggest, however tentatively, something to replace the argument that I have criticized, and this I will now do.

120

Actually, developing an alternative explanation will not be all that difficult, as I fully believe that the general theory that Professor Douglas presents is entirely correct, although mis-applied in the case of Leviticus. With apologies to Professor Douglas for what must seem to be unconscionable *hubris*, I suggest that what follows is better application of her theory than her own application of that theory.

Consider first the category "swarming things", defined as unclean in Lev. 11:29. The fact that succeeding verses (Lev. 11:32–5) talk about what should be done if these "swarming things" come into contact with food, drink or kitchen vessels has suggested to some biblical scholars[10] that this category refers to those animals that an Israelite would likely encounter in or around the walls of his dwelling. The modern term for this category would of course be *vermin*. What does the definition of such creatures as "unclean" suggest?

Borrowing a page from Lévi-Strauss, let us assume that people everywhere make a distinction between *nature* and *culture*, and that the world of animals is associated with *nature* and the world of men with *culture*. Now consider vermin: these are animals (*nature*) that invade the world of men (*culture*), by contaminating their food and infesting their dwellings. Under this interpretation "swarming things" (vermin) is a category that blurs the borderline between *nature* and *culture*. On the hypothesis that such borderline categories become the object of ritual taboos (which is the Douglas theory), the definition of "swarming things" makes perfect sense.

Now consider the list of twenty specific birds defined as unclean in Lev. 11:13–19. Douglas[11] says she can say nothing about this list because there are no descriptions associated with the various birds named and the translation of many of the names is open to doubt. Without denying that some of the names are uncertain, there is enough specificity about the list to have suggested to some scholars[12] that most of the prohibited birds are either birds of prey (e.g., eagle, hawk, falcon, etc.) or carrion eaters (e.g., vulture). In short, the prohibited birds seem to be *carnivorous* birds.

To understand the significance of all this it is necessary to go back to Genesis. Although it has probably escaped the attention of most modern readers, Gen. 1:30 makes it quite clear that God initially intended all living creatures, including man to be vegetarians:

> And to every beast of the earth, and to every bird of the air, and to everything that creeps upon the earth, everything that has the breath of life, I have given every green plant for food.

121

Only after the Flood, in establishing a covenant with Noah and his descendants, did God lift this vegetarian requirement, and even then, it was lifted *only* for men:[13]

> Every moving thing that lives shall be food for you; and as I gave you the green plants, I give you everything. (Gen. 9:3)

In other words, within the logic established in Genesis, "meat-eating" is appropriately associated only with men (and thus *culture*) and is not associated with animals (*nature*). Within this framework, meat-eating animals are a class of things that blur the *nature/culture* distinction, and thus the definition of carnivorous birds as unclean is perfectly consistent with what Douglas' theory would lead us to expect.

But as mentioned earlier, the "flying creature" category includes not only birds, but also winged insects. Is the hypothesis being suggested here consistent with what Leviticus has to say about this latter category? In answering this, consider the following list, which is a list of the winged insects most often mentioned in the OT:[14] 1. locusts, 2. grasshoppers, 3. moths, 4. flies, 5. gnats, 6. bees, 7. hornets.

While winged insects are generally classed as unclean (Lev. 11:20), locusts and grasshoppers are specifically exempted from this prohibition (Lev. 11:21–3). Why the exemption for locusts and grasshoppers? It turns out that of all the flying insects listed above, *only* locusts (often mentioned in the OT in connection with agricultural destruction) and grasshoppers are associated exclusively with the eating of plants. All the others (save the moth) are "meat-eaters" in some sense of the word: gnats bite, bees and hornets sting and most authorities[15] suggest that OT "flies" were mainly (like gnats) biting insects. But "carnivorous" flying insects blur the *nature/culture* distinction in the same way that carnivorous birds blur this distinction, and thus should also be defined as unclean. If the list given above does roughly exhaust the main categories of winged insects known to the Israelites, then Leviticus' general prohibition against winged insects, with the specific exception of locusts and grasshoppers, establishes the uncleanness of small flying "carnivores" in just the way that the list of birds in Lev. 11:13–19 establishes the uncleanness of large flying carnivores.

Moths do not eat meat, but they do eat the garments of men (something which the OT recognizes on several occasions). Since "clothing" is part of the world of *culture*, the moth can be viewed as an animal that blurs the *nature/culture* distinction in its own way.

What about land animals? It has already been noted that the prohibition of animals "that go down upon their paws" refers to animals that have pads upon their feet. The Hebrew text is also quite clear in dictating that *wild* animals are being referred to here.[16] If we reflect upon what types of "wild animals with pads upon their feet" tend to be mentioned in the OT, we find that these also turn out to be carnivores (e.g. lions, bears, wolves, etc.).

This same idea is expressed in a more positive manner by the rule (Lev. 11:3) which defines as clean those land animals that chew the cud and part the hoof. Virtually, all the animals that meet this criterion are *grass-eating* ungulates. Meat-eaters – like the omnivorous pig – that possess only one of these attributes (e.g. parted hooves) are not clean, as Lev. 11:4–8 makes it clear that both of these attributes must be present.

On the other hand, I do not see how the argument being developed here can fully account for the fact that Leviticus defines as clean only those water creatures with "fins and scales". Thus, for example, "eels" and "shellfish" – both defined as unclean by this rule – do not in any obvious way blur the *nature/culture* distinction. But considering fish only, this argument does suggest an interesting perspective upon the "fins and scales" rule, where the "and scales" might at first seem redundant.

If modern readers were asked to name a carnivorous fish, most would undoubtedly name some variety of shark. While I can locate no source which suggests that the ancient Israelites were familiar with sharks, it is the case that several varieties of shark are today found in the Mediterranean.[17] In any case, although sharks have fins, they lack scales. If the intent then was to define carnivorous fish as unclean, then clean fish would have to be defined as those possessing both fins *and* scales.

Although the concern to this point has been entirely with the dietary rules in Leviticus, in fact such rules are part of a larger system. Leviticus defines uncleanness not only as it applies to animals (Lev. 11), but also uncleanness as it applies to childbirth (Lev. 12—13), to leprosy (Lev. 14), and to bodily discharges (Lev. 15).

As to bodily discharges, Leach[18] has already suggested that such discharges (including, for instance, semen, menstrual blood, feces, etc.) are almost universally tabooed because they threaten another major distinction (besides *nature/culture*), this being the distinction between *self* and *outside world*. If we assume that childbirth also threatens this same distinction, then Leach's explanation (which is itself an application of Douglas' general theory) would seem perfectly capable of accounting for the "uncleanness" rules relating to childbirth and bodily discharges in Leviticus.

This leaves only the rules dealing with leprosy. It is clear that "leprosy" is a generic term in Leviticus that refers to more than just the modern disease that we know by that name, if only because Leviticus devotes separate sections to each of three different types of leprosy:

1. leprosy that infects people (Lev. 13:1–45),
2. leprosy that infects garments (Lev. 13:47–59),
3. leprosy that infects buildings (Lev. 19:33–53).

From the description of the symptoms that Leviticus gives in connection with "garment" and "building" leprosy, it is generally concluded that what is being referred to is mould and mildew.[19] Since mould and mildew are both forms of plant life, what is being defined as unclean here are plants (which belong to *nature*) and invade the world of man (*culture*), by infesting his garments and his dwellings. Here again then what is being defined as unclean is a category of things that blurs an otherwise sharp distinction between *nature* and *culture*. (In fact, mould and mildew can be seen as the plant kingdom's equivalent to "vermin", already defined as unclean in Lev. 11:29–38.)

While the leprosy that Leviticus mentions as infecting individuals probably includes a variety of skin diseases, certainly the most notable such disease would be the one that we today call leprosy. It seems plausible to suggest that the physical deformities induced by this disease also blur the *nature/culture* distinction by distorting the "human" appearance of the person so afflicted. This interpretation receives some textual support from Leviticus itself.

For instance, leprous individuals are required (Lev. 14:46) to dwell "outside the camp" (though obviously this by itself could be explained in purely hygienic terms). More telling is the requirement (Lev. 14:45) that a leper "shall wear torn clothes and let the hair of his head hang loose". Since clothing and dressed hair clearly belong to *culture*, this requirement can be seen as reflecting the leper's disassociation from *culture*.

Conclusion

I have argued that Leviticus defines as unclean those things anomalous with respect to the *nature/culture* distinction, either because they are animals that eat meat (a prerogative that Genesis assigns to men only) or because they are things – like vermin, mould or mildew – that properly belong to *nature* yet invade the world of man. Although this argument cannot account for the entire list of unclean animals in Leviticus, this was also true of Douglas' original argument (which could not, for instance, account for the list of prohibited birds). The advantages of the present argument over that developed by Douglas are (*a*) that it is more consistent with the actual text in Genesis and Leviticus, and (*b*) that it accounts not simply for the dietary regulations, but also for the larger set of regulations (including those relating to leprosy) of which the dietary regulations are but a part.

But in the end, I too have linked uncleanness to anomaly, and that after all is the general theory that Douglas proposed. I would like to think that in validating that general theory the contribution of this chapter has been more positive than negative.

NOTES

1 Mary Douglas, *Purity and Danger* (London: Routledge & Kegan Paul, 1966) 41–57 [= ch. 6 of this volume].

2 M. Douglas, *Implicit Meanings* (London: Routledge & Kegan Paul, 1975) 276–314.

3 James Strong, *The Exhaustive Concordance of the Bible*, 21st edn (New York: Funk & Wagnalls, 1874) 29. The Hebrew term is *dagah*.

4 *The New Westminster Dictionary of the Bible*, ed. Henry Gehmann (Philadelphia: Westminster Press, 1970) 118. The Hebrew term is *'oph*.

5 Douglas, *Purity and Danger*, 56 [= p. 114 of this volume].

6 Douglas, *Purity and Danger*, 56 [= p. 114 of this volume].

7 The Hebrew term is *yad*.

8 Martin Noth, *Leviticus. A Commentary*, ET (London: SCM, 1965) 95; Norman Snaith, *Leviticus and Numbers* (London: Nelson, 1967) 86.

9 James Hastings, *Dictionary of the Bible*, rev. edn (New York: Charles Scribner's Sons, 1963) 188.

10 Snaith, *Leviticus and Numbers*, 87.

11 Douglas, *Purity and Danger*, 55 [= p. 114 of this volume].

12 *Peake's Commentary on the Bible*, ed. Mathew Black, H. H. Rowley (London: Thomas Nelson, 1962) 247.

13 [Editor's note: This view that the text of Genesis implies the idea of vegetarianism before the deluge has been recently challenged by L. Dequeker, "Green Herbage and Trees Bearing Fruit (Gen. 1:28–30; 9:1–3): Vegetarianism or Predominance of Man over the Animals?", *Bijdragen* 38 (1977) 118–27.]

14 Based upon the discussion in J. Feliks, "Animals of the Bible and the Talmud", in *Encyclopaedia Judaica*, vol. 3, 7–19 (Jerusalem: Keter, 1971) 18.

15 *Encyclopaedia Biblica*, ed. Thomas K. Cheyne, J. S. Black (London: A. & C. Black, 1915) 1537; *The New Westminster Dictionary of the Bible*, 305.

16 Snaith, *Leviticus and Numbers*, 86.

17 H. McCormick, T. Allen, W. Young, *Shadows in the Sea* (Philadelphia: Chilton Books. 1963).

18 Edmund Leach, "Anthropological Aspects of Language: Animal Categories and Verbal Abuse", in *Reader in Comparative Religion*, ed. William A. Lessa, Evon Z. Vogt, 3rd edn, 206–20 (New York: Harper & Row, 1965) 211.

19 *The Oxford Annotated Bible, with the Apocrypha*, ed. Herbert G. May, Bruce M. Metzger (New York: OUP, 1965) 138, 140.

8

*Genesis Restructured**

MICHAEL P. CARROLL

Up to this point, the analysis has been for the most part negative in that it has focused upon the weak points in Leach's analysis.[1] It is only fair that I now be called upon to do something positive, and this section will therefore present my own efforts to apply structuralist principles to Genesis. No new theoretical ground will be broken here, and in fact the whole point will be to demonstrate that structural principles that have been used in other contexts can indeed be fruitfully applied to Genesis.

Central to the whole Lévi-Straussian outlook is the proposition that, because of certain innate limitations, the human mind is capable of conceptualizing only a limited number of structural patterns, and that the patterns in this limited set are related to one another by a series of logical "transformation" rules. Virtually all of his recent work on mythology[2] is an attempt to validate this perspective by considering a set of myths and by showing that each myth in a given set can be transformed into some other member of the set. Two of the "transformation rules" that have been proposed by structuralists will form the basis of the discussion here.

The Internal Structure of Individual Myths

1 Cain and Abel

In his original work on myth, Lévi-Strauss proposed that a myth could be transformed into one of its variants using the following rule:

> With two terms, *a* and *b*, being given, as well as two functions, *x* and *y*, of these terms, it is assumed that a relation of equivalence exists between two situations defined respectively by an inversion of *terms* and *relations*, under two conditions: (1) that one term be replaced by its

*First published in *AE* 4 (1977) 663–77.

opposite ... (2) that an inversion be made between the *function value* and the *term value* of the two elements (... y and a).[3]

I must confess that I have never been completely certain of the meaning of this passage. Reviewing the many transformations that he actually makes, I would like to suggest that his original rule is simply an overly general formulation that Lévi-Strauss uses to subsume several different transformation rules, and that in fact the following represents one of the more precise rules so subsumed:

> *Transformation Rule 1.* Starting with two roles, X and Y, which are related to each other in a particular way,
> 1(*a*) negate the outcome associated with each role, and then
> (*b*) move the actor originally in one of the roles, say X, into role Y, and move a new actor into role X.

What I now want to show is that this transformation rule underlies much of the *internal* structure of the Cain and Abel myth. Consider the following elements:

> (A) Abel ritually sacrifices the firstborn of his flock.
> (B) The sacrifice is accepted by God.
> (C) Abel dies.

Now apply the transformation rule, assuming that the two roles are "sacrificer" (= X) and "sacrificed" (= Y). The first part of the rule necessitates that the outcomes associated with each role be negated, which means that "accepted" in event (B) becomes "rejected" and that "dies" in event (C) becomes "lives". The second half of the rule suggests that the actor "Abel" be moved from the role "sacrificer" to the role "sacrificed" and that a new actor (say, "Cain") be moved into the role of "sacrificer". The events are now:

> (D) Cain ritually sacrifices Abel.
> (E) The sacrifice is rejected by God.
> (F) Cain lives.

Putting all the events (A) through (F) together produces most, though not all, of the elements in the first half of the Cain and Abel myth.

Some comment is necessary, however, because event (D) – "Cain ritually sacrifices Abel" – might at first sight seem a quite forced reading of the text in Genesis. Certainly the common impression is not that Cain ritually sacrificed Abel, but that Cain acted on impulse and simply murdered his brother. Nevertheless, most readers overlook the fact that Cain specifically asks Abel to "go out to the field", and the inference drawn by at least one biblical scholar is the following:

> It is in the *field*, the tilled soil whose infertility has brought about the situation, that the slaying of Abel takes place, and the suggestion is that ... the slaying was a ritual one, not an impulsive murder instigated by jealousy, but a ceremonial killing intended to fertilise the soil by drenching it with the blood of the victim.[4]

2 *The Fall of Man*

As another example based on the same transformation rule, consider the Genesis account of the fall of man. The key roles here would seem to be "tempted" ($=X$) and "tempter" ($=Y$). Thus:

(A) The serpent (tempter) asks Eve (tempted) to eat the forbidden fruit.
(B) Hostility is established, by a command of God, between the tempter and the tempted, that is, between the serpent and Eve (Gen. 4:15: "I will put enmity between you and the woman").
(C) Eve (tempted) is made subordinate to her spouse.

Applying the transformation rule would mean that "hostility" in (B) would become "attraction" (that is, some force driving tempted and tempter together, rather than driving them apart), and "subordinate" in (C) becomes "superordinate". The second half of the rule necessitates moving Eve from the role of "tempted" to the role of "tempter" and introducing a new term "Adam" into the vacated role. This produces:

(D) Eve (tempter) asks Adam (tempted) to eat forbidden fruit.
(E) Attraction is established, by a command of God, between tempter and tempted, that is, between Eve and Adam.
(F) Adam (tempted) is made superordinate to his spouse.

Taken together, these six elements – (A) through (F) – account for most of the elements that compose the Genesis myth relating to the fall of man.

The only event that might need clarification is event (E). In his curse (Gen. 3:16), God tells Eve three things: that she will suffer pain in childbirth, that she will be subordinate to her husband, and that "your desire shall be for your husband". This last phrase is usually taken to mean that Eve will have a strong sexual attraction for her spouse.[5] What I am suggesting is that by acting as a form of attraction between tempter and tempted, "sexual desire for" is here the negation of the "hostility" between tempter and tempted in event **(B)**.

To be sure, the present analysis has not dealt with all the elements in either the account of Cain and Abel or the account of the fall. Thus, for instance, nothing has been said of the fact that Cain's initial sacrifice (of cultivated plants) was rejected, or that Eve was cursed with the pains of childbirth. But in arguing that one myth can be transformed into another, Lévi-Strauss has never meant to say that every single element of a given myth is transformed into some corresponding element in the second set. After establishing that the myths in some set are transformations of one another, he always finds something that is left over, that is, elements from the various myths under considerations that are not yet accounted for in the analysis. In fact he argues that his firm methodological rule is to begin a new analysis by considering the "residue" left over from the preceding analyses.[6]

The goal in this section has only been to show that for at least two myths in Genesis, part of their internal structure can be subdivided into two segments, one of which is a transformation of the other. There is much that is left over in each myth, and in fact the next section will begin (according to Lévi-Strauss' "rule") by considering some as yet unanalysed portions of the Cain/Abel myth.

Incest and Exchange

I begin by assuming that "fratricide" represents (in the extreme) the "undervaluation of close kin relations", and asks what follows upon such an undervaluation in the story of Cain and Abel. What follows (in Gen. 4:17–24) is that Cain first becomes a wanderer, then in short order (1) acquires a wife, (2) has a son, (3) founds the first city, and is then (4) identified as the ancestor of herdsmen, forgers of bronze and iron, and of those who play the pipe and lyre. In other words, after the fratricide and subsequent wandering, Cain acquires a wife and becomes associated with cities, the domestication of animals, blacksmiths, and musicians – all of which indicate a relatively advanced cultural state.

To those familiar with Lévi-Strauss' early work on kinship,[7] this should all sound a bit familiar. In that work, the central theoretical problem for Lévi-Strauss was the origin of "culture". More exactly, he was concerned with determining how "culture" developed from "nature". His answer was that the foundation of culture is the incest taboo, in that this forces exogamy (the need to find a marriage

130

partner outside one's own kin group), and an exogamy rule in turn promotes the exchange of women among the various kin groups in a society. The solidarity among various kin groups that such an exchange promotes is the precondition for the development of culture.

It does little violence to Lévi-Strauss' basic argument to restate it in the form of two propositions, each of which is the mirror image of the other:

(1) The devaluation of close kin relations promotes the exchange of members among different social groups, and this exchange is the basis for the development of culture.
(2) The overvaluation of close kin relations (represented in the extreme by incest) does not promote the exchange of members among different social groups and is associated with the absence of culture.

These two propositions are slightly more general than Lévi-Strauss' own theory because he restricts his attention to the exchange of members among different unilineal kin groups as a result of patrilineal or matrilineal exogamy rules. These two propositions allow for the possibility that the devaluation of close kin relations might promote the exchange of members – not simply among different unilineal kin groups – but also among different local communities or among different cultural groups, and that any of these exchanges (and not simply the exchange of members among different unilineal kin groups) might produce "culture".

What I now want to argue is that these two propositions represent not simply a theory developed by a twentieth-century social scientist but are also the principles that generate the structure for many (most, in fact) of the myths in Genesis. These two principles give rise to two basic mythological structures, each of which can be related to the other, using a very simple transformation rule.

The first structure, which is a specification of the first proposition, is simply:

(A1) An event occurs that indicates the devaluation of a close kin relationship.
(A2) One of the individuals involved in this relationship is forced to move from his local community and as a result comes into contact with the members of a new community.
(A3) The individual acquires a wife from this new community and becomes associated with "cultural" elements.

There are several myths in Genesis that exhibit this basic structure. As already implied, the first is the Cain/Abel myth:

(1) Cain kills his brother Abel.
(2) Cain is forced to wander among various communities (hence the need for a mark to signal his divinely protected status and thus protect him from harm).
(3) Cain acquires a wife and becomes associated with cities, the domestication of animals, blacksmithing, and music.

The same pattern is found in the story of Jacob and Esau (Gen. 27—32):

(1) Esau plots to kill his brother Jacob (because Jacob used trickery to obtain the blessing of their father Isaac, which rightfully belonged to Esau).
(2) Jacob flees to the country of his mother's brother, Laban the Aramean, in order to be out of Esau's reach.
(3) Jacob obtains two wives (Laban's daughters, Leah and Rachel) from this community and over the years acquires much wealth, mainly in the form of domesticated livestock.

The final example is taken from the story of Joseph:

(1) Joseph's brothers came to hate Joseph (primarily because Joseph was the most beloved of their father Jacob) and plot to kill him.
(2) Plans are changed, and instead of killing him, they sell Joseph to some travelling traders, with the result that Joseph ends up in Egypt.
(3) After some initial tribulations, Joseph wins the favour of Pharaoh, who gives Joseph both a wife (the daughter of an Egyptian priest) and authority over the entire Egyptian state (one of the most powerful civilizations in that era).

A second set of myths all share a pattern that can be produced from events (A1) through (A3) using a transformation rule outlined by Leach in his work on the "legitimacy of Solomon".[8] Leach argues that the story of Jepthah in Judg. 11:30–40 can be transformed into the story of Abraham in Gen. 22:1–18 by first applying the rule "substitute each element with its binary opposite" and then reversing the order of events in the myth. Whether or not he can do what he claims is not certain. For instance, his analysis involves the assumption that the binary opposite of "virgin daughter" is "virgin son" (why not nonvirgin daughter?), and that the binary opposite of "father" is "God" (why not "mother?").

But whatever the status of his own analysis, the following will be adopted as our second transformation rule:

Transformation Rule 2. Given a sequence of events, negate the outcome of each event and reverse the ordering of the events.

Applying this to events (A1) through (A3) produces our second basic pattern:

(B1) "Culture" is lost (not acquired).
(B2) If the actor(s) move at all, it is not movement that brings him (or them) into contact with members of other communities.
(B3) Some event occurs that indicates the overvaluation of close kin relations (typically this means incest).

This basic structure – (B1) through (B3) – underlies at least two of the stories in Genesis, the first being in the story of Noah (Gen. 6—8):

(1) God destroys all of human civilization with a flood.
(2) Noah and his family float – in isolation – upon the flood waters in their ark.
(3) After the flood has subsided and the family unit has re-established itself on dry land, Noah gets drunk and is seduced by his son Ham.

Homosexual incest between Ham and his father Noah is being inferred from the statement (Gen. 9:22) that Ham "saw the nakedness of his father". In his own comment on the Noah myth, Leach[9] says that this phrase consistently refers to sexual intercourse in the Old Testament, yet in fact this is only one of several meanings that the phrase can have.[10] The interpretation that incest occurred is thus a plausible, but by no means certain, rendering of the text.

The second myth having the structure (B1) through (B3) is that concerning Lot and the destruction of Sodom and Gomorrah (Gen. 20:24–38):

(1) God destroys the cities of Sodom and Gomorrah.
(2) Lot and his family flee to the safety of an isolated cave (his wife being lost along the way).
(3) Lot is seduced in turn by each of his daughters (because they think that their father is the last man on earth).

Towards the end of his later article, Leach[11] argues that Genesis emphasizes close kin endogamy by indicating that those who practice such endogamy, even when it borders on incest, are favoured. Since this might sound similar to my own argument, I would like to indicate briefly how the two arguments differ.

The two arguments direct one's attention to different aspects of the same story. For instance, in considering the story of Jacob and Esau, Leach focuses upon the fact that Jacob (his father's favourite) married two Israelite women while Esau married a non-Israelite. Note that this latter event (Esau's marriage) did not figure in my own analysis of the same story. However, my analysis did focus upon an event, namely, the devaluation of close kin relations evident in the quarrel between Jacob and Esau, that does not figure in Leach's analysis. Furthermore, while Leach would argue that incest or near incest (at least among Israelites) is associated with relatively favourable outcomes, my analysis suggests that incest (as an instance of the overvaluation of close kin relations) should be associated with the destruction of culture. In short, the two arguments are quite different, though there is no particular reason why they could not be viewed as complementary to one another.

In summary then, this section has tried to establish (1) that each of the five myths under consideration (dealing respectively with Cain, Noah, Lot, Jacob, and Joseph) has one of two structures, that is, each myth conforms either to (A1) through (A3) or to (B1) through (B3); (2) that these two basic structures can be transformed into each other using a transformation rule already in the structuralist literature; and, finally, (3) that one of these structures – namely (A1) through (A3) – is nothing less than a version of Lévi-Strauss' own theory relating to the social effects of the exchange of members among different social groups. Of course, if one wanted to be really clever, one could say that Lévi-Strauss' theory is simply another version of a myth that occurs quite frequently in the OT.

Conclusion

The first half of this article showed that many of the interpretations made by Leach in his analysis of Genesis are not justified by the text of Genesis. But whereas Thomas *et al.*,[12] in their criticism of the ethnographic interpretations that underlie Lévi-Strauss' analysis of the Asdiwal myth, seem to mount an attack on structural analysis in general, that has not been the goal here. Structural analysis is a powerful and quite novel way of discovering interrelated cognitive patterns underneath a wide variety of myths. The goal of the second half of this article was to demonstrate this by using modifications of already established structuralist principles to find common patterns beneath many of the familiar stories in Genesis.

NOTES

1 The first part of Carroll's paper "Leach, Genesis, and Structural Analysis", not reproduced here, is devoted to a criticism of Edmund Leach's structuralist interpretations of parts of the book of Genesis.

2 Claude Lévi-Strauss, *The Raw and the Cooked*, ET John and Doreen Weightman (New York: Harper & Row, 1969); *From Honey to Ashes*, ET J. and D. Weightman (New York: Harper & Row, 1973).

3 C. Lévi-Strauss, *Structural Anthropology*, ET Claire Jacobsen *et al.* (New York: Basic Books, 1963) 228.

4 S. H. Hooke, "Genesis", in *Peake's Commentary on the Bible*, ed. Matthew Black, H. H. Rowley, 175–207 (London: Nelson, 1962) 181.

5 Cf. *The New Oxford Annotated Bible with the Apocrypha*, ed. Herbert G. May, Bruce M. Metzger (New York: OUP, 1973) 5 note.

6 Lévi-Strauss, *From Honey to Ashes*, 22.

7 C. Lévi-Strauss, *The Elementary Structures of Kinship*, ET J. Bell *et al.* (Boston: Beacon Press, 1969).

8 Edmund Leach, *Genesis as Myth* (London: J. Cape, 1969) 38.

9 Leach, *Genesis as Myth*, 19.

10 E. A. Speiser, *Genesis*. The Anchor Bible (Garden City, N.Y.: Doubleday, 1964) 61.

11 Leach, *Genesis as Myth*, 19–22.

12 L. L. Thomas, J. Z. and D. B. Kronenfeld, "Asdiwal Crumbles: A Critique of Lévi-Straussian Myth Analysis", *AE* 3 (1976) 147–73.

9

*The Logic of Sacrifice**

EDMUND LEACH

I

How could structuralist theory help the anthropologist to understand what is going on when he or she encounters a totally unfamiliar chunk of culturally defined behaviour?

The present chapter applies the theory to the procedures of sacrifice. This seems an appropriate test case because, although animal sacrifice is a very common feature of religious ritual, most of my readers will have had no first-hand acquaintance with such performances. If we now examine the details of a description of a sacrifice, how far does the theory in fact help to elucidate what is going on?

The central puzzle about sacrifice centres around the metaphor of death. What has the killing of animals got to do with communication between man and deity or with changing the social status of individuals? My own immediate problem is of a different kind. How can I describe enough of the total context of a typical sacrificial rite for you to get some feeling of the complexity of the problems which face the anthropological analyst when he meets with such performances in the field? For you must understand that in any fieldwork situation many things are going on at once. At the very least, any ritual activity has visual, verbal, spatial and temporal dimensions; in addition, noise, smell, taste, touch may all be relevant. Many action sequences will probably be repeated several times over but often with slight variations at each repetition. How then should the observer discriminate between the significant, the accidental and the redundant?

First let me review the theory as such. The argument hitherto suggests two rather different models of how religious ritual serves to express a relationship between the world of physical experience and the other world of metaphysical imagination.[1]

*First published in *Culture and Communication* by Edmund Leach (1976) 81–93.

136

Model I was schematized in an earlier diagram[2] which I reproduce, with different wording, as Fig. 1. The concept of the other world is generated by direct inversion of the characteristics of ordinary experience. This world is inhabited by mortal, impotent, men, who live out their lives in normal time in which events happen in sequence, one after another. In this world we get older and older "all the time" and in the end we die. The other world is inhabited by immortal, omnipotent gods, who exist perpetually in abnormal time in which past, present and future all coexist "simultaneously".

In this first model "power", conceived as the source of health, life, fertility, political influence, wealth ... is located in the other world and the purpose of religious performance is to provide a bridge, or channel of communication, through which the power of the gods may be made available to otherwise impotent men.

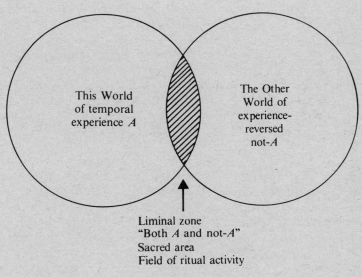

This World
of temporal
experience A

The Other
World of
experience-
reversed
not-A

Liminal zone
"Both A and not-A"
Sacred area
Field of ritual activity

Fig. 1

This world and the other world are here conceived as separate topographical spaces separated by a liminal zone which partakes of the qualities of both. It is the liminal zone which is the focus of ritual activity (e.g. churches, graveyards, shrines). The metaphysical "persons" to whom the ritual activity is addressed are associated with these sacred places and are typically regarded as ancestors, saints, or incarnate deities – beings who were formerly ordinary men who died ordinary deaths but who have now become immortal gods. Like the liminal zone itself they partake of qualities drawn both from this world and the other world.

The human beings who perform the ritual activities are likewise abnormal by the criteria applied to ordinary mortal men. They may be *priests*, who are required to put themselves into a special condition of "ritual purity" before they can undertake the main ritual, or they may be *shamans*, spirit mediums who have acquired an abnormal capacity to put themselves into trances, in which state they are supposed to communicate directly with beings from the other world.

The alternative Model II is represented by Fig. 2.[3] The emphasis here is on metaphysical time rather than metaphysical space or semi-metaphysical persons. Social time is made to appear discontinuous by inserting intervals of liminal, sacred non-time into the continuous flow of normal secular time.

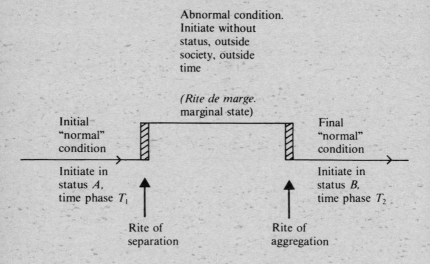

Fig. 2

According to this second model the purpose of ritual activity, which need not necessarily have an explicitly religious form, is to bring about a transition from normal to abnormal time at the beginning of the ceremony and another transition from abnormal to normal time at the end of it.

The two models are complementary rather than contradictory and either or both may in practical situations throw light on the structure of observed ritual performances and the purposes that lie behind them.

So how about animal sacrifice?

One view, which quite often appears to be supported by the language in which people describe their own sacrifices, is that a sacrificial offering is a gift, or tribute, or fine paid to the gods. The performance is an expression of the principle of reciprocity. By making a gift to the gods, the gods are compelled to give back benefits to man.

Model I suggests that part of the logic by which men should come to suppose that killing an animal constitutes a gift to the gods depends upon the following metaphorical associations. The souls of dead men pass from the normality of this world to the abnormality of the liminal zone, and then, by further transformation, become immortal ancestor deities in the other world. If we want to make a gift to a being in the other world, the "soul", that is to say the metaphysical essence, of the gift must be transmitted along the same route as is travelled by the soul of a dead man. We must therefore first kill the gift so that its metaphysical essence is separated from its material body, and then transfer the essence to the other world by rituals which are analogous to those of a funeral.

At one level this does seem to be how people think about their sacrifices, though the metaphor of gift giving can easily prove misleading. Gods do not need presents from men; they require signs of submission. The material body of the sacrificial victim may well be a serious economic cost to the giver of the sacrifice, but, at the metaphysical level, economics is not the issue. What matters is the act of sacrifice as such, which is indeed a symbol of gift giving, but gift giving as an expression of reciprocal relationship rather than material exchange.

In point of fact, as a rule, most of the meat of the slaughtered animal is eaten by members of the "congregation", who are friends and relatives of the giver of the sacrifice. When this is not the case the animal is likely to be small, or to be replaced by something else of trivial economic value, e.g. there are circumstances when the

Nuer (as described by Evans-Pritchard) will replace an ox by a wild cucumber!

In any event, the animal or object sacrificed is a metonymic sign for the donor of the sacrifice. By arranging for a liminal priest to perform the sacrifice in the liminal zone, the donor provides a bridge between the world of the gods and the world of men across which the potency of the gods can flow (toward himself).

Model II suggests a slightly different set of metaphors. As before and as in all rites of transition the paradigm is provided by mortuary ritual. At death a living man becomes, by the process of "natural" *separation*, a dead corpse plus a ghost-soul. This separation is treated as a "purification" of the ghost-soul, which is initially deemed to be in limbo, separated from, but still close to, its original domestic environment. But whereas the soul has been purified, that from which it has been separated – i.e. the corpse and the close kin of the deceased – has become polluted.

After an interval, further rituals aggregate the ghost into the category of ancestors and bring back the polluted mourners into normal society by removing their pollution. The general utility of this model is shown by the frequency with which the metaphor of death and rebirth crops up in all sorts of initiations.

The paradigmatic idea is that the procedures of the rite *separate* the "initiate" into two parts – one pure, the other impure. The impure part can then be left behind, while the pure part can be aggregated to the initiate's new status. In the case of sacrifice the sacrificial victim plays the part of the initiate, but since the victim has first been identified with the donor of the sacrifice, the donor is, by vicarious association, likewise purified and initiated into a new ritual status.

From this point of view the sacrifice is a magical act which moves the whole proceedings on to the next stage. The aura of sacredness which surrounds the act of killing ties in with the fact that sacrifices are markers of boundaries in social time.

II

I propose now to apply this general theory to a specific piece of purported ethnographic description which is readily available to everyone.

The biblical story of the consecration of Aaron as high priest, which appears in two very similar versions in Exodus and Leviticus, provides a detailed account of sacrificial procedures of a kind that can still be observed at first hand in all sorts of different ethnographic contexts throughout the world. It explicitly brings sacrifice into association with a rite of transition and it also gives special emphasis to the use of sacrifice as a means to the attainment of ritual purification through separation from impurity.

In these biblical stories the ethnographic context is mythological: the Israelite Tabernacle, as described in the text, is culturally, architecturally and archaeologically an impossibility. But the very precise details of the associated rituals are certainly not imaginary. The myth served as a justification for Jewish sacrificial practices associated with the Temple at Jerusalem around the third century B.C. At the point in history when the stories were first committed to writing the various categories of behaviour which are distinguished must have corresponded to ethnographic facts which were known to the author at first hand. The similarity to sacrificial procedures which I have myself witnessed in various parts of South East Asia is indeed quite remarkable.

So my suggestion is that you treat these texts "as if" they represented the notebook record of a contemporary ethnographer. Get hold of a copy of the Bible and, in reading my analysis, check back constantly to the original text as you might well want to do if I were referring to a modern anthropological monograph. Where sacrificial procedure is concerned my main references are to Leviticus chapters 1—10 and 16. Part of this text is very similar to Exodus chapter 29. Various details in Exodus chapters 28 and 30 are also relevant.

The meticulously detailed description of the construction of the Ark and the Tabernacle in Exodus chapters 25—27 needs to be viewed rather differently. It is a model for the layout of a setting for sacrificial procedure, a representation of cosmological space as shown in Fig. 3. This point calls for elaboration.

First of all you have to remember that every religious ritual, no matter whether it takes place at a wayside shrine temporarily erected for the purpose or in a permanent setting such as the sanctuary of a cathedral, is performed within the confines of a stage, the boundaries and segments of which are artificial. At a structural level the components of such stages are highly standardized. There are three essential elements:

Zone 1 The shrine proper, which, in the context of the ritual, becomes extremely sacred. It usually contains some iconic symbol which makes it immediately apparent that this is where the deity

141

is, e.g. an image, an empty seat, a crucifix ... In the context of the ritual this "shrine proper" is treated as if it were actually part of the other world.

Zone 2   The place of assembly of the congregation. The essential point here is that this area must be close to but separated from the shrine proper. In the context of the ritual, ordinary members of the congregation must not enter the shrine proper, which is reserved for priests and other religious functionaries.

Zone 3   An area of middle ground on which most of the action of the ritual takes place which is likewise reserved for the priests.

For example, in the context of an uncomplicated form of the Christian communion service, the "shrine proper" is the altar, the "place of assembly of the congregation" is the whole of the church to the west of the altar rails, "the middle ground" is the area between the altar and the altar rails. In terms of Fig. 1, Zone 1 corresponds to the right-hand circle, Zone 2 to the left-hand circle, Zone 3 to the liminal area common to both.

Every particular case however will be a variation on this basic theme and, in the biblical stories, the model by which the empirical setting of the ritual is transformed into cosmological space is somewhat more complicated. It is these additional complications that I have tried to indicate in Fig. 3.

If you are to understand how the diagram fits the story you will need to pay close attention to what is said in the Exodus references about the construction and lay-out of the Tabernacle and to various cross-references to this design in Leviticus chapters 4, 5 and 6. Although the Taberbnacle is represented as a tented structure the authors clearly had in mind a temple building, the groundplan of which would have been not unlike that of many Christian churches but oriented to the north rather than to the east.

The precise position of the shrine area in relation to the secular camp is not specified but the implication seems to be that the Taberbnacle stands at the centre of the camp which is regarded as the zone of normal culture, a domesticated tame area contrasted with "outside the camp", the wilderness zone of wild nature.

The shrine area as a whole is fenced off from the camp by a rectangular arrangement of hangings (Exod. 27:9–17). The entrance is on the south side and marked with curtains of bright colours. At the centre of this "court" is a much more substantial structure with wooden framed walls and tented roof (Exod. 26). The entrance to

Cosmological space categories	Text categories	
Wild Nature	Outside the camp	
Tame Culture	Inside the camp	
Intermediate Zone *A* Relatively secular	Court of Tabernacle	⎡ Place of assembly ⎤
Threshold between This World and the Other World	Altar Permanent fire	⎡ Middle
Intermediate Zone *B* Relatively sacred	Tabernacle (south side) Table, candlestick	
Final Limit of This World	Curtain	ground ⎤
Other World	Tabernacle (north side) Mercy Seat Ark	⎡ Shrine proper ⎤

Fig. 3

the tent, similarly marked with bright colours, is again on the south side, and immediately in front of it, in the court, is the altar. This is an elaborate hearth on which a fire, tended by the priest, burns perpetually. The tented structure itself is in two parts divided by a curtain. To the north the holy of holies contains the Ark of the Covenant and the Mercy Seat. To the south of the curtain, and thus between the Ark and the altar, is an intermediate sacred area containing the table and the candlestick (Exod. 26:33–5).

In addition to these various localities inside the camp, there is a vaguely specified "clean place" somewhere outside the camp, in the wilderness, on which the priest deposits the ashes from the altar fire and other materials which are sufficiently contaminated with sacredness or "dirt" to be too dangerous to retain within the camp.

The whole of the area within the Taberbacle proper is exclusively reserved for the priests, who must be properly attired and in a ritual state of purity whenever they are tending the altar fire or in the building to the north of it. The restrictions applying to the northern half of the tented area, beyond the curtain, are even more severe.

Great stress is placed upon the details of the priest's dress as a distinguishing mark of his ritual condition. When the priest carries the ash from the altar to the "clean place outside the camp" he must also wear special clothes, but of a different kind.

Ordinary lay members of the congregation who wish to participate in a ritual may enter the untented "court of the Tabernacle" but may not pass beyond the altar. All transactions between the lay donor of a sacrificial offering and the altar must be mediated by a priest.

The compatibility of the left half of Fig. 3 with this description is, I hope, clear. In terms of metaphysical topography, the camp represents this world, the holy of holies represents the other world. The intermediate zone, which is the focus of active ritual attention is in two sections, the court (Zone A) which is relatively secular and free of taboo and the south side of the Tabernacle (Zone B) which is relatively sacred and loaded with taboo. The altar, around which most of the ritual of the Tabernacle is concentrated, stands between these two parts of the intermediate zone; it is thus the threshold marking the topographical transition from normal to abnormal, this world to other.

The fire of the altar is the gateway to the other world, the channel through which offerings can be transmitted to God, but also the channel through which the power of God can be directly manifested to man (Lev. 9:24; 10:2).

So much for the setting, but now let us examine the structure of the rituals for which the setting provides a frame. The early chapters of Leviticus are largely concerned with providing prototype rules for the conduct of various types of sacrifice.

Notice how the same elements of ritual behaviour keep on recurring, but linked together in different combinations and different sequences. The elements are like the letters of the alphabet; in different combinations they can be made to say different things.

Leviticus chapter 1 spells out the details of three types of *burnt sacrifice*. The basic difference in the types is in the ranking (i.e. economic cost to the donor) of the victim: (i) a bullock, (ii) a ram or male goat, (iii) a pigeon. In each case the victim's blood is sprinkled around the altar and the door of the Tabernacle and the carcass is cut into portions. The portions are allocated to two categories, (i) an offering, (ii) a residue. The offering consists essentially of the kidneys and the surrounding fat, though in the case of the pigeon it consists of everything except the crop and the feathers. The offering portion is always burnt on the altar; the residue is variously treated. In these particular examples the residue is washed clean of the contents of the stomach and guts (which are put with the ashes of the altar fire) and then burnt.

Chapter 2 describes the procedure for making *"a meat offering to the Lord"*, which turns out to be a food offering to the priest. The animal is not ritually killed, but a share of meat from a household meal is mixed with ritual oil and flour and frankincense and handed over to the priest; the priest then takes a token portion of the food and burns it on the altar fire. Notice that it is not only the right of the priest to eat this food, it is a duty; for once the food has passed into the hands of the priest it is contaminated with sacredness and too dangerous to take back again into the camp.

Chapter 3 introduces a category called *peace offering*. The procedure for killing the victim is the same as in chapter 1 and the carcass is similarly apportioned, but here only the blood and the offering are handed over to the priest. By implication the donor keeps the rest for himself. However in this chapter certain points about the general procedure are more clearly spelled out. Before the sacrificial animal is killed the donor of the offering invariably establishes a metonymic relationship between himself and the victim by touching the victim on the head. The plain implication is that, in some metaphysical sense, the victim is a vicarious substitution for the donor himself. Notice further that in 3:17, the composition of the "offering" portion is used as justification for a general taboo on the eating of fat and blood by members of the Jewish faith.

Chapter 4 discusses *sin offerings* and the role of sacrifice in ritual purification. In this case the distinguishing criterion appears at verse 11. The residue, which was burnt on the altar in chapter 1 and retained by the donor in chapter 3, is here treated as highly contaminated and removed *in toto* to the "clean place outside the camp" where it is burnt among the ashes from the altar fire.

But now let me go back to the mythological account of the consecration of Aaron and his sons which is given in Leviticus 8— 10. Pay close attention not only to who does what to whom but also the order in which the sequence of events is presented. The story presupposes the cosmological–ethnographic context which I have already described. There is a good deal of redundancy and repetition but almost every detail exemplifies one or other of the abstract theoretical principles which have been considered in earlier sections of this essay.

To show this I will lead you through the story verse by verse:

LEVITICUS (CHAPTER AND VERSE REFERENCE)
CHAPTER 8:4 The congregation assemble at the door of the Tabernacle (Fig. 3, intermediate zone A).

6 The potential initiates (Aaron and his sons) are separated from the congregation and washed with water. Notice that at this stage Moses, who is already established as a preist–mediator who can communicate directly with God, acts as master of ceremonies.

7 Aaron, as principal initiate, is separated from his sons and dressed in special regalia which are specified in detail.

10 The whole of the interior of the Tabernacle, and then the altar and the associated ritual utensils, are sprinkled with ritual oil which is then sprinkled also on Aaron's head (i.e. Aaron is brought into metonymic association with the holy things on the altar). Notice that the anointing and sprinkling with oil is analogous to the sprinkling of the blood of the sacrificial victim.

13 The secondary initiates (Aaron's sons) also are dressed in special clothes.

14 The bullock of the sin offering is then produced and Aaron and his sons touch the head of the bullock with their hands.

15–17 Moses sacrifices the bullock in accordance with the rules laid down in chapter 4.

18–21 Moses sacrifices "the ram for the burnt offering" in accordance with the rules laid down in chapter 1. The bullock (sin offering) of verse 14 and the ram (burnt offering) of verse 18 need to be seen as a linked pair, analogous to the pair of pigeons in Lev. 5:7–10. The two sacrifices are similar but different; the overall implication is the already redundant theme of "separation", especially separation of purity from impurity.

You may here find it useful to look back at Fig. 2. We have now completed the initial "rite of separation".

22 A further ram is now produced which is described as "the ram of consecration". Here the identification of the ram with Aaron and his sons is pursued even more systematically than before (verse 24) but when the "offering" portion of the victim's carcass has been separated it is not burnt in the usual way by the priest, but is first handed over to Aaron and his sons. After the initiates have waved the dish containing the offering over the altar, Moses, as priest,

takes it back again and its contents are then burnt as before.

29 Moses himself goes through a similar "waving" performance with the "breast" of the ram – i.e. with a part of the carcass that would otherwise be treated as "residue" – but does *not* burn it.

30 A further anointing with oil and blood repeats the same message – Aaron is identified with the *offering* portion of the victim's carcass, *not* with the *residue*.

31 Moses now hands over the meat of the "residue" to Aaron and his sons and instructs them to cook and eat this within the confines of the Tabernacle and to stay in confinement there for seven days. Here look again at Fig. 2. We have now reached the end of the *rite de marge* and the newly consecrated priest must be brought back into society in his new social status by a rite of aggregation.

CHAPTER 9:1–4 There is a further series of sacrifices paired as before (see comment on 8:18–21 above):

(i) a sin offering (young calf) }
(ii) a burnt offering (ram) } with Aaron as donor

(iii) a sin offering (kid goat) }
(iv) a burnt offering (calf and lamb) } with the whole congregation as donor

(v) a meat offering (verse 17) }
(vi) a peace offering } for the whole congregation

The proceedings are the same as those described in chapter 8 with the difference that Aaron now performs all the priestly functions which had previously been assigned to Moses.

The culmination comes at verse 24 where the effectiveness of Aaron's priestly ministrations is shown by the fact that "a fire came out from before the Lord and consumed the burnt offering and fat upon the altar". This manifestation of divine power is appropriately accompanied by noise – "the people shouted".

But remember that, according to the mythical–metaphysial representation of the proceedings, Aaron himself is the victim who has been transmitted to the other world to establish a channel of communication with the deity, so in order to get back again to normality in his new priestly status, Aaron must sacrifice (shed by separation) a part of himself.

CHAPTER 10:1–7 So the myth has the two sons Nadab and Abihu destroyed by the fire of the Lord. Their bodies are not treated as normal human corpses but as the residue of a sin offering, i.e. they are taken outside the camp without ceremony. That this myth expresses the idea of purification through sacrifice rather than divine retribution is made clear by the fact that the imperfect sons Nadab and Abihu are promptly replaced by perfected sons Eleazar and Ithamar (verse 12). Moreover the account of the destruction of Nadab and Abihu (verses 1–5) is immediately followed by a homily on the importance of putting a "difference between holy and unholy and between clean and unclean".

Incidentally this structuralist view which makes Eleazar and Ithamar a "replacement" of Nadab and Abihu rather than separate characters provides an explanation for the otherwise puzzling argument of 10:16–20. The "sin offering in the holy place" which Eleazar and Ithamar fail to eat is, by substitution, the bodies of their dead brothers, or by further substitution, themselves!

I want you now to skip a few chapters and take a close look at Leviticus 16, which describes the procedure for the sacrifice of the scapegoat. The point that I want you to appreciate is that this seemingly anomalous form of sacrifice is simply a transformation of what has been described before which fits in with the same set of cosmological ideas and the same set of metaphoric and metonymic associations.

The basic theme is that, since God himself is liable to be present on the Mercy Seat in the holy of holies, even Aaron as high priest can only enter the northern end of the Tabernacle (Fig. 3) after specially elaborate rituals of purification.

Five sacrificial animals are involved altogether:

(i)   a sin offering (bullock) ⎫
(ii) a burnt offering (ram) ⎭ with Aaron as donor (verse 3)

(iii) a sin offering (two goats) ⎫ with the whole congregation
(iv) a burnt offering (a ram) ⎭ as donor (verse 5)

The special feature in this case is that the two goats in (iii) are first distinguished by chance – that is by divine intervention (verses 8–10) – and then differently treated. The general procedure with the animals *other than* the goat which has been selected as scapegoat (verse 8) is the same as before, except that the blood sprinkling is specifically stated to extend into the holy of holies and to include the Mercy Seat, but the scapegoat is the object of a special ritual (verses 21–2). By means of a magical verbal spell the sins of the congregation are collectively transferred to the goat. The goat is then taken away into the uninhabited wilderness and abandoned alive.

The other goat and the bullock are treated as ordinary sin offerings as in chapter 4 (see above).

Taken as a whole the scapegoat sequence is the exact converse of the Aaron sequence. Aaron, separated step by step from the secular contaminations of the congregation and his own imperfections, ends up pure and holy at the centre of the camp. The scapegoat, having been separated step by step from other goats and other sacrificial animals, is loaded with the contaminations from which the congregation and Aaron have been freed and then ends up impure and unholy (but nevertheless "sacred") far out in the wilderness.

The central principle is that the separation of spiritual essence from material body at death is paradigmatic of the mechanism which "causes" a change of social status among the living. The repeated use of animal sacrifices to mark stages of transition in all kinds of rites of passage exploits this paradigm.

But conversely, in the scapegoat case, we need a symbol for a creature which is removed from the ritual stage but is *not* separated from its impurities. It is therefore appropriate that the scapegoat should *not* be killed.

I hope I have persuaded you that, in the analysis of ethnography, attention to small details really matters.

Some of you may wonder how far, if at all, these very general interpretative statements can be applied to Christian rituals.

Sacrifice in Christianity appears only in vicarious symbolic form as a reference to mythology. According to the myth, the God-man Christ was murdered by men of evil intent. But by a complex transformation this has retrospectively become a sacrifice, in that the murder was willed by God. The sacrifice is now a persisting channel through which the grace of God can flow to the devout believer. The donor of the sacrifice is Christ himself and the priest, in offering the bread and wine to the congregation as "the body and blood of Christ", is, by implication, timelessly repeating the sacrifice at the behest of the divine Donor.

Because we happen to know a great deal about the history of Christianity we can see that the cross-references and symbolic transformations in this particular case have been exceedingly involved. The Christian Mass, as a whole, is a transformation of the Jewish Passover, and the crucified Christ "is" the sacrificial paschal lamb, "the Lamb of God". The bread and wine are on this account associated with the meat of the sacrifice not only by metaphor but also by metonymy (cf. Leviticus 23).

These issues are extremely complex but even so I would point out that the metaphor, which I have analysed, whereby Aaron himself has to suffer the pangs of sacrifice before he can become fully effective as a permanent intermediary between God on his Mercy Seat and the sinful suffering congregation, is structurally very close indeed to the Christian idea that Jesus must die before he becomes fully effective as a permanent mediator between God and suffering mankind.

The theological literature on the subject is vast but anthropologically naïve. Anthropological analysis of a modern kind is sparse. A paper which adopts, in some respects, the terminology of this present essay is by Fernandez.[4]

NOTES:

1 Edmund Leach, *Culture and Communication* (Cambridge: CUP, 1976) 33ff., 51ff., 77ff.

2 Leach, *Culture and Communication*, 35.

3 [Here inserted from Leach, *Culture and Communication*, 78.]

4 J. W. Fernandez, "The Mission of Metaphor in Expressive Culture", *CA* 15 (1974) 119–45.

10

*An Interpretation of Sacrifice in Leviticus**

DOUGLAS DAVIES

The last thirty years have witnessed a marked development in the
study of anthropology and in our understanding of symbolism,
myth and the place of ritual both in religion and ordinary social
life such that problems incapable of formulation by W. Robertson
Smith but which H. Hubert and M. Mauss approached in a more
systematic way, may now be studied with a greater hope of success.
While E. Durkheim's perspective remains of great significance to
the study of religion, it is to the methodology of what has come to
be called structuralism that this paper is directed. The term itself
is not easy to define but indicates an area of interest in the human
mind and its systematic ordering of social institutions and the
natural world of man's environment. It is a way of looking at
questions concerning human nature, social structure, myth and
symbolism which has been closely associated with the French
anthropologist C. Lévi-Strauss, but which also has its British
advocates in E. Leach, Mary Douglas and others less well known
to the general public.

Some eight years ago Mary Douglas in her book *Purity and
Danger* provided an analysis of the dietary prescriptions of Leviticus
in terms of the way in which the Israelites classified their world.
She showed that the catalogue of peculiar creatures which were not
to be eaten was not constructed on an arbitrary basis, but according
to quite intelligible rules. Because of this, Mary Douglas was able
to demonstrate that this one aspect of Israelite life mirrored a
broader attitude to the world rather than being a piecemeal
exhortation on how to avoid stomach upsets in the wilderness. It
is our aim to develop this approach and to apply it to the institution
of sacrifice as described in Leviticus. Questions of Pentateuchal

*First published in *ZAW* 89 (1977) 388–98.

criticism are largely avoided in this immediate context both because of the complexity of the issues involved and since, as R. de Vaux has shown, it does not resolve the basic problem of the significance of sacrifice.[1] Our aim is to provide one framework within which sacrifice in Leviticus may be understood; more specifically, it focuses upon the sin and guilt offerings as central rites in the book, while acknowledging that other offerings may have diverse origins and significance prior to the Levitical redactions. In *Purity and Danger* Mary Douglas considered the problem of pollution and ritual purity in Leviticus in a wide context of the social life of Israel, on the assumption that any single aspect of a social structure is better understood in the light of many others. One dimension which was not considered was that of the idea of covenant, an unfortunate omission which, because of its obvious social implications in morality and ethics, will merit attention in due course. For the purpose of this study Leviticus is viewed as a post-exilic compilation expressing the world view of the nation's religious leaders and incorporating their understanding of the nature and identity of Israel and the gentile world. This image may well be ideal and rather removed from the reality on the ground, yet it represents the prevailing understanding of those practices viewed as central to the life of the nation, in particular the ritual of sacrifice. Leviticus expresses a national feeling which is basically self-oriented and concerned with those within the society; the experience of the exile and the more remote history inevitably meant that the nation must be self-conscious in a way in which, for example, a preliterate society relatively isolated from other communities is not. This self-consciousness and its association with sacrifice and in particular the ritual of atonement, has been recognized by OT scholars; "the whole nation became a priesthood for one day" in the passover rites which constituted "so deeply national an institution" lying at the heart of the national consciousness.[2]

Covenant and Codes

The basis of this self-awareness and identity of Israel lay in the covenant established between God and the people, a covenant central to which was the sacrificial ritual, and basic to which were firm ethical expectations both with respect to the nation's status vis-à-vis God, and the relations of man to man. Accordingly, we may think of the holiness of the nation in terms of these ordered social relationships, an orderliness and perfectness which mirrored the perfection of God so that just as the goodness of the creation in Genesis 1, which is also a Priestly document, lies in its ordered state as opposed to the state of chaos, so the social life of Israel is only "good" when its social network of relationships is ordered. This process of ordering involves the question of ethics and morality, in that one function of sacrifice in Israel is the maintenance of the moral life of the nation in a balanced condition.

Mary Douglas has already suggested that the dietary codes of Leviticus exemplify God's holiness and perfectness through the ordering of the natural world into recognizable categories which serve as a model for and as a symbolic expression of the unity and completeness of God; "holiness is completeness" and is manifested in society through the ordering of chaos.³ By contrast, W. Robertson Smith viewed the laws of uncleanness as irrational survivals of an older set of taboos, and the offering of unclean animals during the period of national calamity when the "national religion appeared to have utterly broken down" as a return to primitive totems.⁴ The modern scholar who works from a structuralist position views these categories not as irrational survivals, but as the outworking of the order-conferring processes of the human mind at work in social institutions; similarly the offering of profane creatures during a crisis period might be understood in terms of the reversal of normal behaviour and values, a reversal paralleling the upheaval of normal social life. If we extend this general argument to include the area of morality which Mary Douglas tends to ignore, we may suggest that just as the priests were to be physically perfect men whose bodies symbolized wholeness and perfection, as was also the case with the victims, so the nation was to be internally harmonious as God worked through it his purposes of election and salvation. In this covenant union, some consideration must be given to the part played by, or believed to be played by God, as well as to the functions of the priests and other Israelites. Against this background of covenant we can see that H. Hubert and M. Mauss were correct in regarding sacrifice as a means of communication between parties, or rather, between different worlds, and we shall adopt this idea with the qualification necessary in the specific case of Israel, that it is better to regard the mediation between the sacred and profane realms as performed by the priesthood rather than by a sacrificial victim.

At this point a brief word on methodology will be useful, for one problem which arises when the mechanics of sacrifice is discussed in terms of gift and communion theories is that nineteenth- or twentieth-century ideas are easily imposed upon the thought forms of pre- and post-exilic Israel. For example, H.-J. Kraus says that the "earliest and original expression of sacrifice is that of giving".[5] This evolutionist assumption of an outmoded kind is only a little less conjectural than his statement that "the one who offers the sacrifice pays homage to the *deus praesens*, submits himself to him and demonstrates his complete devotion".[6] This latter assertion also illustrates a second problem, the error of psychologizing, from which modern anthropology has decidedly turned, but which constituted the methodology of the discipline from the late eighteenth century until the early decades of the twentieth. Its goal was to reconstruct the intention, emotion and aim of the worshipper from the evidence of rituals performed and practices employed. E. E. Evans-Pritchard parodied this approach by calling it the "if I were a horse" mentality; this desire to think oneself into the situation of a former generation might further be described as constituting introspection at a distance.[7] This is a hazardous task, fraught with the possibility and likelihood of error, not only because men vary in their temperaments and religiosity as W. Robertson Smith astutely observed,[8] but because modern researchers have themselves found it very difficult to assess an individual's intention and emotion in religious matters even when the subject is available for questioning. The variety of interpretations of a rite given by participants is often great and betokens the caution due in this approach. While any theorizing over the significance of the atonement ritual or sacrifice in general will involve certain presuppositions, the structuralist framework adopted here is a little more secure than the often-used method of historical conjecture over origins, both because it may be compared with studies of religion carried out by modern anthropologists, and also because it is acknowledged that the rites concerned constitute what might be called a constructed ritual as opposed to a naturally occurring rite which might be found in a preliterate group. Much as modern liturgies are constructed from elements of earlier rites under the influence of a contemporary theological emphasis, so the priestly developments emerged from items of more ancient practice under the formative presence of theological concerns. The only justification for attempting a new analysis of the Levitical ritual is that the biblical literature is a given account of practices which have not been completely understood by the theories of sacrifice put forward in the late nineteenth and early twentieth century, and that in a structuralist analysis we have the means of understanding what certain social acts and patterns of behaviour mean. We are not dependent upon seeking the origin

154

of the rites or of ascribing certain acts to other, neighbouring groups from which borrowing took place or diffusion of practices occurred, as is sometimes done, neither do we depend on the sort of argument which asserts that the accounts of the rituals do not contain an explanation of the events and that the meaning of the rites must have been commonly known, and accordingly needed no explanation.[9] By contrast we presuppose that the form the rites took, their symbolic patterning, itself gives the meaning, though it is necessary to view the rites within the wider context of the idea of covenant as already indicated above.

In coming to consider sacrifice within this social context we may begin by viewing transgression as possessing two aspects, one relating to the offender who was thrown out of proper relationship both with God and his fellow men, and the other to God the offended one, whose integrity or holiness might be brought into question if his covenant partners were permitted to do whatsoever they willed. Theologically speaking, sacrifice is concerned with both of these aspects, but this present study only takes up the social dimension, though at certain points it is difficult to separate the two aspects of the problem. W. Robertson Smith had been careful to explain that in early society the gods were thought of as intimately associated with men, both being members together in one society or social communion. By this he was attempting to indicate the part played by gods in the social life of men, and to indicate that ordinary acts could be seen to possess another dimension involving the sphere of action of a divinity. In the sense that references to gods came into decision-making and motives for behaviour, one might say that the world in which a group lived was shared with a god or gods. So it was for Israel, that if individuals entered a state incongruent with good relations with God, they had to undergo rites to restore them to a normative status; similarly, a person who wronged his neighbour or the nation itself needed to be subject to a ritual of restoration. Within the network of relationships of Israelite society we may identify at least five categories of interaction, each of which was potentially dangerous to the society at large, in that if any one became internally fragmented then the whole state of balance and unity of the group was affected to a greater or lesser extent, and the covenant relationship itself might be threatened. These categories may be arranged in pairs of oppositions, and though we shall consider only the first and last in any detail all could be analysed in a similar way.

God   — Nation
God   — Priesthood
God   — Israelite
Israelite — Israelite
Israelite — Nation

Before analysing these relationships it should be noted that some theologians have recognized the importance of this social dimension even though they have not been able to provide a suitable analytical framework; for example, H. H. Rowley argues that "all sin is sin against the society of which the sinner is a part", and that "where sin was ritually conceived, it was capable of ritual removal". Similarly he argues that "daily offerings [were made] on behalf of the community so that right relations might be maintained between it and God";[10] even so H. H. Rowley provides no substantial theoretical explanation for the assertions, and this we must now attempt through a study of the ritual of the Day of Atonement.

Atonement Ritual

To clarify the following analysis, this continuum has been constructed which will help to illustrate the relationship between central features of rites.

Sacred			Profane
God	Priesthood	People	Gentiles
Temple		Camp	Wilderness
Life			Death
Being	Transient	Existence	Nothingness
Order		RITUAL	Chaos

In the atonement ritual all earthly things, including priest and altar, were located at the profane pole thereby accentuating the otherness, holiness and transcendence of God in contrast to sinful man, while the potential danger to the priests caused by God's presence also signified his immanence. It also indicated that the high priest was associated with the sinful on this day, which is why he divested himself of the gold garments, which, along with everything else which normally was set apart for divine use, were now profane. The nature of the covenant as an agreement between parties of different categories became clearer as their respective moral characters were acknowledged and the terms of reference reasserted. This dangerous state of ritual chaos came to an end and the natural order was restored after the immolation of the one goat for the nation's sin and the sending of another into the desert; the change was symbolized by the revesting of the high priest prior to the burning of the slaughtered victim. In other ritual contexts the priests and altars are located at the sacred pole and serve to mediate the holy to the people who remain within the impure sector. One context in which they were neither sacred nor profane but in a transitional state was that of ordination when they ate their own offerings on the border between the "tent and camp".[11] We may now understand other aspects of the atonement ritual such as the significance of the goat sent into the wilderness, and we need not identify Azazel with the spirits of the wild but merely interpret the symbolism of the continuum. The goat, then, passed through the people after having been identified with the sins of the nation, and was led into the desert, not into the "dumping ground for Jewish sin", but rather from the realm of ordered society, from the holiness of the Tabernacle into the chaos, into the symbolic nothingness which obtained outside the community of God's people.[12] In one sense the goat no longer existed, for the wilderness did to it what the fire did to the remains of the slaughtered victim. In both cases a movement occurs from one pole to another of the continuum, and in the process a readjustment takes place in the status and relationships existing among those symbolically associated with the victims by the laying on of hands and the confession of sin.[13] Destruction overtook both victims as the one drew too close to the divinity and the other too far away; they both passed through the normal boundaries of the social world. In the sacrifice, the ideas both of expiation and propitiation are involved, in that the high priest was not to appear before God without a sacrifice for his own sin, lest he also die. It is possible, as is usually argued, that the immolated animal vicariously represented both the sinners and the nation, and received in its death a punishment for their sin, but this is not explicit. What is explicit is that there is life in the blood and that the sacrificial use of this blood is able to restore normal relationships between God and the people. By referring to the continuum we may hypothesize that blood, which symbolizes life and represents the covenant, may also be associated with order and the divine aspect of life. So it is that in chapter 17 of Leviticus the people are to acknowledge God as the life-giver when they kill an animal, rather than make of it an offering to some other deity or destroy it as an irrelevancy. There can be no final answer to some of these questions involving blood, since powerful symbols of this kind often operate on several different levels of meaning, some of which may no longer be available to us in the Levitical literature.[14]

The priest, as the representative of the nation, involved the whole people in sin if he transgressed. His sacrifice of a bull whose remains were burned outside the camp in a "clean place" was similar to the demands made on the whole community if it sinned.[15] Contrariwise, a single leader offered only a goat which was not burned outside the camp. The ritual state of the priest and the mode of disposal of the victim is a significant point in that the other priests might eat the sacrifices brought by Israelites for their private sins in the sin and guilt offerings, but might not eat their personal sacrificial meat. Similarly, priests might not partake of offerings made at their own ordination. These patterns of activity may be understood in the light of the foregoing analysis since when they were representing God to others they were ritually pure and able to cope with or dispose of the offerings of the people, but when their own sin was involved they were impure and impotent as priests. This interpretation is more plausible than N. H. Snaith's evolutionist argument that "this cereal offering was different from all others in that the whole was burnt on the altar. The rite is of the utmost importance since it is a survival of the day when [the grain offering] was truly the tribute of agriculturalists".[16] Similarly the death of the high priest served to remove sin which found no other form of forgiveness in Israel. Having been set apart for divine service during his life he might be regarded as being in a group of sacred things in the sense of being one who restored confused categories.[17] A particularly good example of the function of sacrifice in this sense of restoring categories and reordering social relations rather than being a means for the removal of sin and guilt, may be seen in the case of lepers, and having considered the atonement rite which represented the relation of God and the nation, the first of our initial pairs of oppositions in the social network of Israel, this example will illustrate the last set of oppositions, the relationship of individual and community.

The problem posed for social stability began with the carefully timed observation of the suspect leper and his exclusion from social life, his peripheral status being indicated by style of hair, clothing and the shout of "unclean".[18] The leper was then viewed much as the creatures in the dietary prescriptions, as an anomalous creature outside the intended order of the world; it is only because he initially belonged to the people of God that such exclusion could effectively take place, for we learn that gentiles and resident aliens do not contract uncleanness, neither do their houses.[19] The elaborate anointing which follows the healing served to remove the person from his status of seclusion into a position of social fellowship within the community, but also served to reposition him within the natural categories of the world which are most clearly exemplified by the social relationships of society.[20] The "leper's" re-entry is set in the form of two phases, the first consisting of the anointing with blood from an animal sacrificed "outside the camp", and which, on our hypothesis, may be explained as occurring because the candidate is, at that point, located outside structured society and cannot, accordingly, benefit from sacrifice performed at the altar which exists at the heart of the social world to serve full members of the same. It would, perhaps, be excessively conjectural to suppose that the blood is life-conferring or covenantal in effecting the readmission, but once he is admitted a second sacrifice takes place, but this time at the altar. As a result of this rite he regains full status as a social person and indicates the same by his dress. A further observation on the outcast nature of the leper may be made from the fact that the earliest phase of reincorporation makes use of intermediaries other than the officiating priest.[21] With respect to the two pigeons used in the restoration rites, we may compare them with the two goats of the atonement rites; the release of the one pigeon which was first dipped in the blood of the sacrificed bird may be seen as effecting a similar function to that of the scapegoat, in that it carried away into the outside world the problem afflicting the man and society. That a similar ritual took place for a house which had some sort of mould is significant, for it further exemplifies the principle that whatever disrupted social life in Israel, as did both leprosy and uninhabitable houses, necessitated ritual action which took the form of sacrifice. It is of further significance that two classes of houses were beyond pollution, those outside Israel and those in Jerusalem, in other words those at the polar extremities of the relationship continuum.[22] In this general case, sacrifice does not involve the notion of moral guilt, whether witting or unwitting, and this reinforces the hypothesis that sacrifice has to do with the correction of social disruption and the reformation of confused categories, as well as involving the problem of sin in other contexts. For the Israelites of the sixth century at least, sacrifice was a focal institution which related to many aspects of life which appear at first to have little in common. As a final example we take the case of the woman's sacrifice after childbirth, for in this instance too, there need be no reference to sin or moral guilt, but merely the fact that after the birth, the woman is readmitted to the ordinary ongoing life of the community. It may be significant that the Mishnah likens the three-phased reincorporation of the leper to that of the woman after childbirth.[23]

Events which led to situations beyond correction in the light of Israel's ethical code require special attention, for these acts, such as murder and adultery, were not subject to sacrificial correction. In ideal terms these social transgressions which disrupted the kinship networks of the people to a marked extent, were only resolved by the death of the offending parties. Douglas has pointed out that both incest and adultery "are against holiness in the simple sense of right order", and one agrees with this but not with the further assertion that "morality does not conflict with holiness ... holiness is more a matter of separating that which should be separated than of protecting the rights of husbands and brothers",[24] for here Douglas overlooks the fact that in Israel morality is inextricably associated with the sacrificial system, as the prophets so often attested. Because sacrifice held the position of a dominant rite it did occur in contexts of what initially appear very different kinds, yet this is no reason for restricting attention to only one form of the rite or one set of meanings. Mary Douglas asserts that her interest lay in the "more negative rules" and not with concerns of love and ethics as outlined in Leviticus 14; this is to be regretted, since the holiness of God in Leviticus is a conception which is expressed in ethical terms as well as in terms of perfection and completeness.[25] Indeed, completeness and perfection is only to be understood in the social action of men and not merely in the choice of specimen animals for sacrifice, which is why atonement is possible only if appeasement and reparation have been made.[26] A failure to work out the implications of this perspective on sacrifice led W. Robertson Smith to say that the idea of uncleanness in Leviticus is not an ethical conception: the truth is that holiness and impurity were not categories which existed in isolation from other phenomena.

Our approach has sought to avoid the problematic areas of individual attention and to focus upon the social dimension of sacrifice in a way which W. Robertson Smith might have favoured but which he was unable to do in his day. Others like H. H. Rowley who, when he said that "it is more likely that the sacrifice was for the ritual cleansing of the leper so that he could take his place in society", came close to adopting an anthropological perspective, have attempted a wider interpretation of ritual in Israel but have not provided convincing arguments.[27] So this chapter offers a modern anthropological interpretation and mode of analysis of the Levitical ritual, and if we accept that the Priestly tradition of which much of Leviticus is thought to consist belongs to that period when post-exilic Judaism was becoming acutely aware of its religious duty and separateness, we may have some further support for the position adopted in seeing sacrifice as an institutional way in which the social and religious life of the nation was both conceived and ordered.[28]

NOTES

1 Roland de Vaux, *Studies in Old Testament Sacrifice* (Cardiff: Univ. of Wales Press, 1964) 101.

2 Philo, De Decalogo 30; G. B. Gray, *Sacrifice in the Old Testament* (Oxford: Clarendon, 1925) 374.

3 Mary Douglas, *Purity and Danger* (London: Routledge & Kegan Paul, 1966) 66.

4 W. Robertson Smith, *Lectures on the Religion of the Semites*, 3rd edn 1927 (New York: KTAV, 1969) 449, 357.

5 Hans-Joachim Kraus, *Worship in Israel* (Oxford: Blackwell, 1966) 113.

6 Kraus, *Worship in Israel*, 115.

7 Edward E. Evans-Pritchard, *Theories of Primitive Religion* (Oxford: Clarendon, 1965) 108.

8 W. R. Smith, *Lectures on the Religion of the Semites*, 28.

9 Gerhard von Rad, *Theologie des Alten Testaments*, vol. 1, 4th edn (Munich: Chr. Kaiser, 1966) 263ff.

10 H. H. Rowley, "The Meaning of Sacrifice in the Old Testament", *BJRL* 33 (1950/1) 74–110; see pp. 89, 92, 95.

11 Lev. 4:26; 5:6; 6:7, etc.

12 Edwin O. James, *Origins of Sacrifice* (London: John Murray, 1933) 201.

13 Lev. 16:21.

14 Victor Turner, *The Forest of Symbols: Aspects of Ndembu Ritual* (Ithaca: Cornell Univ. Press, 1967); and *The Drums of Affliction: A Study of Religious Processes among the Ndembu of Zambia* (Oxford: Clarendon, 1968).

15 Lev. 4:12.

16 Norman H. Snaith, *Leviticus and Numbers* (London: Nelson, 1967) 55.

17 Num. 35:28.

18 Lev. 13:45f.

19 Mishnah tractate *Negaim* 3:1; 12:1; cf. Herbert Danby, *The Mishnah* (London: OUP, 1933).

20 Lev. 14:1.

21 Lev. 14:4f.

22 Mishnah tractate *Negaim* 12:4.

23 Mishnah tractate *Negaim* 14:3.

24 Douglas, *Purity and Danger*, 53 [= p. 112 of this volume].

25 Douglas, *Purity and Danger*, 54 [= p.112 of this volume].

26 Lev. 19; Mishnah tractate *Yoma* 8:9.

27 Rowley, "The Meaning of Sacrifice", 97.

28 This paper was written independently of Edmund Leach, *Culture and Communication* (Cambridge: CUP, 1976). Leach read a draft of this paper and sent me the proofs of his chapter, "The Logic of Sacrifice" [=chap. 9 of this volume], as his book was going to press. While the similarity of analysis is striking, my emphasis on the theological presuppositions of the Levitical redactors, especially in terms of covenant, marks a significant difference.

Bibliography

Aerts, Theodor, "The Old Testament through Melanesian Eyes", *Point: Forum for Melanesian Affairs* 2 (1978) 42–70.

Alter, Robert, "A New Theory of Kashrut". *Commentary* 68/August (1979) 46–52.

Andreasen, Niels-Erik A., "The Role of the Queen Mother in Israelite Society", *CBQ* 45 (1983) 179–94.

Andriolo, Karin A., "A Structural Analysis of Genealogy and World View in the Old Testament". *AA* 75 (1973) 1657–69.

—, "Myth and History: A General Model and Its Application to the Bible", *AA* 83 (1981) 261–84.

Ben-Yosef, I. A., "Jonah and the Fish as a Folk-Motif", *Semitics* 7 (1980) 102–17.

Carroll, Michael P., "Leach, Genesis, and Structural Analysis", *AE* 75 (1977) 663–77. [Included, in part, in this volume as chap. 8]

—, "One More Time: Leviticus Revisited", *AES* 19 (1978) 339–46. [Included in this volume as chap. 7]

—, "Myth, Methodology and Transformation in the Old Testament: The Stories of Esther, Judith and Susanna", *SR* 12 (1983) 301–12.

Carroll, Robert P., *When Prophecy Failed: Cognitive Dissonance in the Prophetic Traditions of the Old Testament.* New York: Seabury, 1979.

Crüsemann, Frank, *Der Widerstand gegen das Königtum.* WMANT 49. Neukirchen-Vluyn: Neukirchener Verlag, 1978.

Culley, Robert C., ed., *Oral Tradition and Old Testament Studies.* Semeia 5. Missoula, Mont.: Scholars Press, 1976.

— and Overholt, Thomas W., ed., *Anthropological Perspectives on Old Testament Prophecy.* Semeia 21. Chico, Ca.: Scholars Press, 1982.

Davies, Douglas, "An Interpretation of Sacrifice in Leviticus", *ZAW* 89 (1977) 387–98. [Included, in part, in this volume as chap. 10]

De Raedt, Jules, "On Freilich's Interpretation of Genesis 1–3", *CA* 17 (1976) 139–42.

Donaldson, Mara E., "Kinship Theory in the Patriarchal Narratives: The Case of the Barren Wife", *JAAR* 49 (1981) 77–87.

Douglas, Mary, "The Abominations of Leviticus", in *Purity and Danger. An Analysis of Concepts of Pollution and Taboo*, 41–57. London: Routledge & Kegan Paul, 2nd edn 1969. Originally published in 1966. [Included in this volume as chap. 6]

163

Bibliography

—, *Implicit Meanings. Essays in Anthropology*, 249–75: "Deciphering a Meal", 276–318: "Self-Evidence". London: Routledge & Kegan Paul, 1975.

Emerton, John A., "An Examination of a Recent Structuralist Interpretation of Genesis 38". *VT* 26 (1976) 79–98.

Flanagan, James D., "Chiefs in Israel", *JSOT* 20 (1981) 47–73.

—, "Succession and Genealogy in the Davidic Dynasty", in *The Quest for the Kingdom of God. Studies in Honor of G. E. Mendenhall*, ed. Herbert B. Huffmon *et al.*, 35–55. Winona Lake, Ind.: Eisenbrauns, 1983.

—, "Social Transformation and Ritual in 2 Samuel 6", in *The Word of the Lord Shall Go Forth. Essays in Honor of D. N. Freedman*, ed. Carol L. Meyers *et al.*, 361–72. Winona Lake, Ind.: Eisenbrauns, 1983.

Frazer, James G., *Folk-Lore in the Old Testament*. 3 vols. London: Macmillan, 1918.

Freilich, Morris, "Myth, Method, and Madness", *CA* 16 (1975) 207–26.

Gaster, Theodor H., *Myth, Legend, and Custom in the Old Testament*. A comparative study with chapters from Sir G. Frazer's *Folklore in the Old Testament*. New York, Harper & Row, 1969.

Gerstenberger, Erhard S. *Der bittende Mensch: Bittritual und Klagelied des Einzelnen im Alten Testament*. WMANT 51. Neukirchen-Vluyn: Neukirchener Verlag, 1980.

Geus, C. H. J. de, "Agrarian Communities in Biblical Times, 12th to 10th Centuries B.C.E.", in *Les Communautés Rurales*, vol. 2 (Paris: Dessain et Tolra, 1983) 207–37.

Girard, René, *Des choses cachées depuis la fondation du monde* (Paris: B. Grasset, 1978) 165–81.

Gottwald, Norman K. *The Tribes of Yahweh: A Sociology of the Religion of Liberated Israel, 1250–1050 B.C.E.* Maryknoll, N.Y.: Orbis, 1979.

Hahn, Herbert F., "The Anthropological Approach to the Old Testament", in *Old Testament in Modern Research*, 44–82. Philadelphia: Muhlenberg, 1954.

Hallpike, C. R., "Social Hair", *Man* 4 (1969) 256–64.

Henninger, Joseph, *Les fêtes de printemps chez les Sémites et la pâque israélite*. Paris: Gabalda, 1975.

Herrenschmidt, Oliver, "Sacrifice: Symbolic or Effective?", in *Between Belief and Transgression. Structuralist Essays in Religion, History, and Myth*, ed. Michel Izard *et al.*, 24–42. Chicago: Univ. of Chicago Press, 1982.

Ifesieh, Emanuel I., "Web of Matrimony in the Bible, Social Anthropology, and African Traditional Religion", *Communio Viatorum* 26 (1983) 195–211.

Jensen, Adolf E., "Beziehungen zwischen dem Alten Testament und der

164

nilotischen Kultur in Afrika", in *Culture in History: Essays in Honor of P. Radin*, ed. Stanley Diamond *et al.*, 449–66. New York: Columbia Univ. Press, 1960.

Jobling, David, "Lévi-Strauss and the Structural Analysis of the Hebrew Bible", in *Anthropology and the Study of Religion*, ed. Robert L. Moore *et al.*, 192–211. Chicago: Center for the Scientific Study of Religion, 1984.

Kippenberg, Hans G., *Religion und Klassenbildung im antiken Judäa.* SUNT 14. Göttingen: Vandenhoeck & Ruprecht, 2nd edn 1982.

Kristeva, Julia, *Powers of Horror: An Essay on Abjection.* ET (New York: Columbia Univ. Press, 1982) 90–112 ("Semiotics of Biblical Abomination").

Lang, Bernhard, "Old Testament and Anthropology: A Preliminary Bibliography", *BN* 20 (1983) 37–46.

—, "The Social Organization of Peasant Poverty in Biblical Israel", in *Monotheism and the Prophetic Minority*, 114–27. Sheffield: Almond Press, 1983. [Included in this volume as chap. 5]

—, "Spione im gelobten Land: Ethnologen als Leser des Alten Testaments", in *Ethnologie als Sozialwissenschaft*, ed. René König *et al.*, 158–77. Kölner Zeitschrift für Soziologie und Sozialpsychologie, Sonderheft 26. Opladen: Westdeutscher Verlag, 1984.

—, "Non-Semitic Deluge Stories and the Book of Genesis: A Bibliographical and Critical Survey", *Anthropos* 80 (1985), no. 4/6.

Leach, Edmund, *Genesis as Myth and Other Essays.* London: J. Cape, 1969.

—, "The Logic of Sacrifice", in *Culture and Communication*, 81–93. Cambridge: CUP, 1976. [Included in this volume as chap. 9]

—, "Anthropological Approaches to the Study of the Bible in the Twentieth Century", in *Humanizing America's Iconic Book*, ed. Gene M. Tucker *et al.*, 73–94. Chico, Ca.: Scholars Press, 1982 [= *Structuralist Interpretations of Biblical Myth*, 7–32].

—, and Aycock, D. Alan, *Structuralist Interpretations of Biblical Myth.* Cambridge: CUP, 1983.

Lemche, Niels Peter, *Early Israel: Anthropological and Historical Studies on the Israelite Society before the Monarchy.* Leiden: Brill, 1985.

Lohfink, Norbert, "Die segmentären Gesellschaften Afrikas als Neue Analogie für das vorstaatliche Israel", *Bibel und Kirche* 38 (1983) 55–8.

Long, Burke O., "The Social Setting for Prophetic Miracle Stories", *Semeia* 3 (1975) 46–63.

—, "Recent Field Studies in Oral Literature and their Bearing on OT Criticism", *VT* 26 (1976) 187–98.

—, "Prophetic Authority as Social Reality", in *Canon and Authority*, ed.

Bibliography

George W. Coats *et al.*, 3–20. Philadelphia: Fortress, 1977.

—, "Social Dimensions of Prophetic Conflict", in *Anthropological Perspectives on Old Testament Prophecy*, ed. Robert C. Culley *et al.*, 31–53. Semeia 21. Chico, Ca.: Scholars Press, 1982.

McFall, Ernest A., *Approaching the Nuer of Africa through the Old Testament*. South Pasadena, Ca.: William Carey Library, 1970.

Malamat, Abraham, "Tribal Societies: Biblical Genealogies and African Lineage Systems", *AES* 14 (1973) 126–36.

Mars, Leonard, "What Was Onan's Crime?", *CSSH* 26 (1984) 429–39.

Marshall, R. C., "Heroes and Hebrews: The Priest in the Promised Land", *AE* 6 (1979) 772–90.

Morgenstern, Julian, *Rites of Birth, Marriage, Death and Kindred Occasions among the Semites*. Cincinnati: Hebrew Union College, 1966.

Niditch, Susan, "The Wronged Woman Righted: An Analysis of Genesis 38", *HTR* 72 (1979) 143–9.

—, *Chaos to Cosmos: Studies in Biblical Patterns of Creation*. Studies in the Humanities, 6. Chico, Ca.: Scholars Press, 1985.

Oden, Robert A., "Transformation in Near Eastern Myths: Genesis 1—11 and the Old Babylonian Epic of Atrahasis", *Religion* 11 (1981) 21–37.

—, "Jacob as Father, Husband, and Nephew: Kinship Studies and the Patriarchal Narratives", *JBL* 102 (1983) 189–205.

Overholt, Thomas W., "Commanding the Prophets: Amos and the Problem of Prophetic Authority", *CBQ* 41 (1979) 517–32.

—, "Seeing is Believing: The Social Setting of Prophetic Acts of Power", *JSOT* 23 (1982) 3–31.

—, "Prophecy: The Problem of Cross-Cultural Comparison", in *Anthropological Perspectives on Old Testament Prophecy*, ed. Robert C. Culley *et al.*, 55–78. Semeia 21. Chico, Ca.: Scholars Press, 1982. [Included in this volume as chap. 4]

Patai, Raphael, *Sex and Family in the Bible and the Middle East*. Garden City, N.Y.: Doubleday, 1959.

Patte, Daniel, ed., *Genesis 2 and 3. Kaleidoscopic Structural Readings*. Semeia 18. Chico, Ca.: Scholars Press, 1980.

Perdue, Leo G., "Liminality as a Social Setting for Wisdom Literature", *ZAW* 93 (1981) 114–26.

Pilch, John J., "Biblical Leprosy and Body Symbolism", *Biblical Theology Bulletin* 11 (1981) 108–13.

Pitt-Rivers, Julian, *The Fate of Shechem, or the Politics of Sex*. Cambridge Studies in Social Anthropology 19. Cambridge: CUP, 1977.

Prewitt, Terry J., "Kinship Structures and the Genesis Genealogies", *JNES* 40 (1981) 87–98.

Proffitt, T. D., "Moses and Anthropology: A New View of the Exodus", *JETS* 27 (1984) 19–25.

Rogerson, John W., "Structural Anthropology and the Old Testament", *BSOAS* 33 (1970) 490–500.

—, "The Hebrew Conception of Corporate Personality: A Re-examination", *JTS* 21 (1970) 1–16. [Included in this volume as chap. 3]

—, *Myth in Old Testament Interpretation*. BZAW 134. Berlin: Walter de Gruyter, 1974.

—, "The Old Testament View of Nature: Some Preliminary Questions", *Oudtestamentische Studiën* 20 (1977) 67–84.

—, *Anthropology and the Old Testament*. Growing Points in Theology. Oxford: Blackwell, 1978. Reprinted: Sheffield: JSOT Press, 1984.

—, "W. Robertson Smith: *Religion of the Semites*", *The Expository Times* 90 (1978/9) 228–33.

—, "Sacrifice in the Old Testament", in *Sacrifice*, ed. Michael F. C. Bourdillon *et al.*, 45–59. London: Academic Press, 1980.

Rooth, Anna Birgitta, *The Raven and the Carcass: An Investigation of a Motif in the Deluge Myth in Europe, Asia, and North America*. FF Communications 186. Helsinki: Suomalainen Tiedeakat, 1962.

Schäfer-Lindenberger, Christa, *Stadt und Eidgenossenschaft im Alten Testament*. BZAW 156. Berlin: Walter de Gruyter, 1983.

Schapera, Isaac, "The Sin of Cain", *IRAI* 85 (1955) 33–43. [Included in this volume as chap. 2]

Smith, William Robertson. *Lectures on the Religion of the Semites*. 3rd edn. Prolegomenon by J. Muilenberg. The Library of Biblical Studies. New York: KTAV, 1969.

Soler, Jean, "The Dietary Prohibitions of the Hebrews", *The New York Review of Books* 26, no. 10 (1979) 24–30.

Steffen, Uwe, *Das Mysterium von Tod und Auferstehung: Formen und Wandlungen des Jona-Motives*. Göttingen: Vandenhoeck & Ruprecht, 1963.

Steiner, Franz, "Enslavement and the Early Hebrew Lineage System: An Explanation of Genesis 47:29–31, 48:1–16", *Man* 54 (1954) 73–5. [Included in this volume as chap. 1]

Thiel, Winfried, *Die soziale Entwicklung Israels in vorstaatlicher Zeit*. Neukirchen-Vluyn: Neukirchener Verlag, 1980, rev. edn 1985.

Westermann, Claus, "Weisheit im Sprichwort", in *Forschung am Alten Testament*, 149–61. TBü 55. Munich: Chr. Kaiser, 1974.

Wilson, Robert R., *Genealogy and History in the Biblical World*. New Haven: Yale Univ. Press, 1977.

—, *Prophecy and Society in Ancient Israel*. Philadelphia: Fortress, 1980.

—, "Enforcing the Covenant: The Mechanisms of Judicial Authority in

Early Israel", in *The Quest for the Kingdom of God. Studies in Honor of G. E. Mendenhall*, ed. Herbert B. Huffmon *et al.*, 59–75. Winona Lake, Ind.: Eisenbrauns, 1983.

—, *Sociological Approaches to the Old Testament*. Philadelphia: Fortress, 1984.

Zuber, Beat, *Vier Studien zu den Ursprüngen Israels*. Orbis Biblicus et Orientalis 9. Fribourg: Universitätsverlag, 1976.

Index of Biblical References

Index of Authors and Subjects

173